Copyright @ 2013 by Dechay Watts, Debbie Williams, and Said Baaghil. All rights reserved.
Published by Content Marketing Institute, a division of Z Squared Media LLC, Cleveland, Ohio.

No part of this publication may be reproduced, stored in a retrieval system, or transmitted in any form or by any means, electronic, mechanical, photocopying, recording, scanning, or otherwise, except as permitted under Section 107 or 108 of the 1976 United States Copyright Act, without the prior written permission of the publisher.

Limit of Liability/Disclaimer of Warranty: While the publisher and author have used their best efforts in preparing this book, they make no representations or warranties with respect to the accuracy or completeness of the contents of this book and specifically disclaim any implied warranties of merchantability or fitness for a particular purpose. No warranty may be created or extended by sales representatives or written sales materials. The advice and strategies contained herein may not be suitable for your situation. Neither the publisher nor the author shall be liable for any loss of profit or other commercial damages, including, but not limited to, special, incidental, consequential, or other damages.

About the Content Marketing Institute
The Content Marketing Institute (CMI) is the leading global content marketing education and training organization. CMI teaches enterprise brands how to attract and retain customers through compelling, multi-channel storytelling. CMI's Content Marketing World is the largest content marketing-focused event. CMI also produces the quarterly magazine, *Chief Content Officer*, and provides strategic consulting and content marketing research for some of the best-known brands in the world. CMI is a division of Z Squared Media, a 2012 Inc. 500 company.

CMI books are available at special quantity discounts to use as premiums and sales promotions, or for use in corporate training programs. To place a bulk order, contact CMI at info@contentinstitute.com or 888/554-2014.

www.contentmarketinginstitute.com

Cover image via Dreamstime.

Library of Congress Control Number: 2013945739

ISBN: 978-0-9859576-2-9

Printed in the United States of America.

BRANDS IN GLASS HOUSES

HOW TO EMBRACE TRANSPARENCY AND GROW YOUR BUSINESS THROUGH CONTENT MARKETING

BY **DECHAY WATTS** AND **DEBBIE WILLIAMS**
WITH **SAID BAAGHIL**

For my parents, whose support gives me the courage to try new things, and for Rich, who keeps the adventure real.
—*Dechay Watts*

For Andy, Cate & Lainey, my loves, daily inspiration, and most authentic part of my life; and for my mother who always encouraged me to be myself.
—*Debbie Williams*

For my "boss," Rakun Said Baaghil, my greatest achievement.
—*Said Baaghil*

Table of Contents

Foreword by Marcus Sheridan......................................11

Introduction...13

CHAPTER 1
EVERY BRAND HAS A STORY…WHAT'S YOURS? 17

What the Heck's a Brand Story?
Every Business is a Brand
Do You Have an Authentic Brand Story?
Making Emotional Connections
How Brands are Telling Their Stories
- Lay's
- Patagonia
- Origins
- Organic Valley

Sheer Advice: How to Uncover Your Brand Story
- Get to the Guts
- Discover Your "Aha!"
- Mind the Gaps
- Audit Your Current Conversations
- Remember, Words Matter

CHAPTER 2
GIVE AWAY YOUR KNOWLEDGE:
BE TRANSPARENT TO BUILD TRUST 39

Connecting Through Content Marketing
How Brands are Giving Away Knowledge
- Sherwin-Williams
- Colgate-Palmolive
- McDonald's Canada

- General Electric
- JetBlue

Everyone Can Play
- The Old World Napa Inn
- CorePower Yoga

Can You Give Away Too Much?

Sheer Advice: How to Give Away Your Knowledge
- Speak Through Your Website
- Ditch the Jargon
- Be a Giver

CHAPTER 3
BE CONSISTENT: TELL THE SAME STORY ACROSS ALL CHANNELS...................... 53

Consistency from the Inside Out
- Zappos
- Target

The Content Lifecycle

Brands that are Consistently Hitting the Mark
- Chipotle
- Grape-Nuts
- Holstee

Inconsistencies in Your Story

Sheer Advice: How to Maintain Consistency
- Create a Content Style Guide
- Create an Editorial Calendar
- Choose the Right Channels

CHAPTER 4
CREATE CUSTOMER AND EMPLOYEE EVANGELISTS: TRUST OTHERS TO DO THE TALKING 71

Why Brand Evangelists?
How They Do It: Brand Evangelists
- Maker's Mark
- Weed Pro Lawn Care

- Aleysai Beverage Corporation
- The Chopping Block
- Lego

Why Employee Evangelists?
How They Do It: Employee Evangelists
- Zingerman's
- FreshBooks

When the Tables Turn

Sheer Advice: How to Create Brand Evangelists
- Define Your Brand Evangelists
- Engage with Influencers
- Listen and Respond!
- Identify Your Partners
- Get Involved
- Treat Your Evangelists Like the Media
- Thank Them

Sheer Advice: How to Create Employee Evangelists
- Accentuate the Positive
- Be a Great Role Model
- Get Out of Their Way
- Create a Community

CHAPTER 5
LISTEN, RESPOND & DEAL WITH NEGATIVITY: HAVE HONEST CONVERSATIONS WITH CUSTOMERS AND YOURSELF 89

Everyone's a Critic
What If?
How They Do It
- KitchenAid
- Domino's Pizza

What Not to Do
- Subway
- Lululemon
- Amy's Baking Company

Sheer Advice: How You Can Do It Right
- Take Your Fingers Out of Your Ears
- Don't Ignore
- Speak Up — Sincerely
- Bite Your Tongue
- Make Sure Your CAPS LOCK is Off
- Don't Take it Personally
- Ask for a Second Chance
- Focus on Good Customer Service Upfront

FINAL THOUGHTS 101

REFERENCES 103

ABOUT THE AUTHORS 105

Foreword

If you don't mind, I want to talk about "reality" for a minute.

Four years ago, the reality for me was simple. Due to the stock market and housing crash, my swimming pool company was going to go out of business. Sixteen employees and their families would be out of work. I was going to lose my home. And never had stress been so great in my life.

It was during that moment of truth that I discovered what today we so often refer to as "content marketing."

But for me, back then, I didn't call it "content marketing." Simply put, the writing was on the wall. The way consumers were shopping had changed. The digital age had mixed with the information age, all leading to a new way of doing things, and my "reality" was that we could either change or become just another failed business in a long line of sinking ships.

So that's what we did. We accepted reality. **We changed.**

On the surface, there was nothing amazing about what we did. We simply altered our philosophy about the way we communicated online. Our motto was simple:

They Ask, We Answer.

In other words, if anyone had ever asked us a question over the years about swimming pools, we were going to answer it on our website. Good, bad, or ugly — it didn't make a difference. Transparency would be the name of the game. Honesty would be the guiding light. The brand was now in a glass house, for all the world to see, and boy did the results astound.

To make a long story short, over time, search engines and consumers alike fell in love with our website — and this meant way more traffic, leads, and sales. We became the ultimate voice of trust within the fiberglass pool industry, and in a period where swimming pool companies have gone out of business left and right, we've managed to survive, thrive, and find financial peace.

I tell you this story in the hopes that, unlike River Pools, you won't have to be going over a financial cliff in order to see the writing on the wall and embrace reality as we know it in the digital age.

We can all see what's happening. It's obvious. And we also know how *we* like to be treated when we visit a website and "interact" with a brand.

That said, to achieve your own River Pools story and become a brand in a glass house, you're going to need a blueprint — which is exactly why this book excites me so very much. When the folks at SPROUT Content asked me to write the foreword for this work, I'll be honest — I was worried it would be just another book filled with theoretical jargon that would leave readers scratching their heads and wondering how to truly get started with a successful content marketing campaign.

I'm happy to say I was dead wrong.

Somehow, in just over 100 pages, the authors have managed to not only paint a vision of effective content marketing through transparency, but they've also loaded the work with multiple real-life examples that are absolutely relatable to any business — big or small, B2B, or B2C.

I sincerely believe that if you embrace the teachings herein, and then follow the plan that has been so neatly outlined, your business will change forever.

Yes, it will be difficult.

Yes, you will experience unique challenges.

But yes, it can be done.

So do it. Become a brand in a glass house and be the best teacher in the world at what you do. Become the voice of your industry. Become the ultimate source for useful information.

By doing so, you'll engender the trust of anyone who sets a digital foot on your website, and the results that follow will likely amaze you — just as they amaze me every single day as I contemplate the magical choice I made to embrace transparency and content marketing four years ago.

Marcus Sheridan
President, The Sales Lion
Co-Founder, River Pools and Spas

Introduction

*"In a time of universal deceit,
telling the truth is a revolutionary act."*
— George Orwell

As a culture, we are fed up with the inauthentic. There are whistle blowers in the financial world and banks are crumbling from dishonesty. Author James Frey was crucified by the media and on *The Oprah Winfrey Show* for exaggerating tales in his best-selling memoir, *A Million Little Pieces*. Journalists such as Jayson Blair and Stephen Glass have fallen from grace after it was proven they had plagiarized or fictionalized facts, quotes, sources, and data. Grassroots organizations like the Environmental Working Group are fighting hyperbole on product labels and demanding change in chemical ingredient regulations.

People want to work with real people. We want to know the people who are mowing our lawns, growing our food, doing our taxes, and offering us insurance. We want honest, easy-to-find information and we reward those businesses that offer it by giving them our purchases, referrals, and loyalty.

Why were we inspired to write this book?

There is a shift underway of being honest and true to who you are. Being real and authentic is even a dominant storyline in mainstream prime-time television. Shows such as *Modern Family*, *Parenthood*, and *The New Normal* fill our living rooms with stories about same-sex parents, surrogacy, sperm donation, stay-at-home dads, teen pregnancy, blended families, adoption, and mental illness. All of these shows depict normal as being the opposite of the status quo, giving people permission to not be afraid to be who they are and live a more authentic life. The idea of hiding who you really are and conforming to an expected standard is not an option anymore. The same is true in business.

Deceit and dishonesty have caused a backlash, a revolution if you will, by people demanding the truth, not only from their neighbors and government officials, but also by the companies with whom they choose to spend their hard-earned money. Consumers don't want to hear generic business speak on websites, cold canned responses to emails or customer inquiries, false exaggerated claims for products, or that your company is "the best," "high quality," or "delivers the greatest results."

"You must be candid and honest with today's discerning and skeptical customers," says our friend Ed Hind, lead principal of Healthy Living Marketing. "You are likely talking to a highly educated audience that tends to be more social and traveled, and has high expectations for transparency. And really, why would you want to be anything other than transparent and candid? It's so much simpler when you can call a spade a spade."

Access to information is growing at an exponential rate and consumers are just beginning to realize the power they have. Businesses are facing a choice: either fight this need for transparency or embrace it.

For years, companies have used advertising to cover up their behavior as people have watched and believed ads. "Fifty years ago, that's where people got their information and their content," says Jeff Rosenblum, founding partner of Questus. "Consumers have taken the power into their own hands. They know if companies are ethical and whether products are good or bad. Consumers have the power. It's a massive paradigm shift."

Oddly, inauthenticity still filters into the marketing and advertising world by agencies and corporate brands alike. Companies make false claims and often intentionally try to misrepresent themselves to look bigger or more experienced than they are. They say they have dozens, hundreds, or even thousands of employees — when really they might have a database of freelancers. Organizations tout a "combined 60 years of experience" of their core team — and showcase logos and names of companies they've worked for in the past — rather than present content that represents who their company really is.

Old school "traditional" marketers still keep everything top secret. They fear that sharing expertise, product development, thought leadership, and insider information will empower customers and their competition — which is exactly what marketers should strive to achieve. If someone doesn't connect with your brand on an emotional level, they won't buy from you, talk about you, share their experience with you, or listen to what you have to say. Companies need to accept the reality that customers are leading the course of brands and the best way to connect is to keep it real.

It has never been more important for companies to step up to the plate, and really rethink their entire marketing approach and how they communicate with the world. Companies are created and run by people who have ideas and a purpose. It's time to share that passion and start conducting business person-to-person.

Brands must open the curtains and lift the veil of "secrecy" to give the world a real bird's-eye view into what makes their companies tick. Even big companies such as McDonald's and General Electric are leaving the B.S. out of business and keeping it real and crystal clear, revealing everything from company financials to failures and how-to successes.

Many brands are setting great examples of how to show your human side through content marketing, social media, and proactive storytelling. They're creating fun, memorable, engaging content that reveals who they are at the core and establishes their credibility with consumers. Content published in blogs, social media, newsletters, e-books, videos, and more provides a window into a company, giving people a glimpse into what the company is about, from "meeting" the people who work there, to learning how products are made and where they come from.

We are here to share these stories with you and show you how being candid and honest about who you are, while sometimes scary, is the only way to do business today.

Chapter 1
Every Brand Has a Story...What's Yours?

"Be yourself. Everyone else is taken."
–Oscar Wilde

What's the first thing you do when meeting someone new? You ask them questions to unveil their story. Where are you from? What kind of work do you do? Do you have children? Do you come here often? Questioning a stranger is more than a polite way to pass time; you're looking for a nugget of information that resonates with you so you can take the conversation to a personal level and find a common ground. You recognize that discernable moment when polite chatter turns into something real, and suddenly you're telling stories about favorite wines, places you've traveled, where you grew up, and the best spots in town for late night cheeseburgers.

Stories make life interesting and give people a way to connect. People crave stories, which creates a big opportunity for brands to tell theirs.

Stories are essential to every business' success. They are the heart of a brand's DNA. Stories make people decide if they like you, if they trust you, if you understand their needs, and if they want to do business with you. Stories leave an indelible mark on people that can last for years to come, continue to grow, and deepen the relationship. You need a story to be a competitor.

If you have any doubt about the power of storytelling, ask participants of The Moth StorySLAM. Novelist George Green started the movement from his New York apartment in 1997 when he gathered a group of friends together to simply tell stories. The idea grew into an organized company that gives real people a platform to tell their personal stories in front of a live audience. Moth storytelling evenings are now held in bars, restaurants, and other community locations in cities including Boston, Seattle, Los Angeles, New York, and Chicago — all because people want to hear stories, and want a chance to tell theirs, too.

WHAT THE HECK'S A BRAND STORY?

A brand story is a communication architecture that tells your company's story from the inside out, enabling you to make emotional connections with your customers to ultimately increase brand awareness, create brand evangelists, and allow your company to profit and grow.

When we talk about brand stories and storytelling, we're not talking about *Dante's Inferno* or *Ulysses*. We are talking about the fundamentals of your business, what makes you different — the foundation of your culture, passions, and missions. We're talking about opening up the "corporate" blinds — or even just your front door — to show the world what you're all about.

A brand story is made up of all that you are and all that you do. From the company's founding, mission, inspiration, goals, audience, and *reason d'etre*, it's why you exist. Your story is made up of the people, places, and ideas that your company thrives on. It's the foundation that keeps a brand going and growing. It's a blend of those vital little nuggets of information about your business, how you came to be, why your products or services are special, what you're passionate about, your company culture, how you make people's lives better in some way, and why you would do business with your company.

A brand story isn't just for the About page of your website; it should trickle throughout every interaction you have with the world. It should shine through in all the content you create and all of your brand marketing efforts. From your website to emails, social media, videos, and even your customer service conversations, your story should be consistently told at every touch point with consumers. Engaging people with your story, and living it every day, is essential for your brand's success and happily ever after. If you don't live your story in all that you do, your story — and your business — will not survive.

EVERY BUSINESS IS A BRAND

Many businesses, especially those in the B2B and service industries, don't even think they are a "brand," let alone have a compelling story. That couldn't be further from the truth and is a big reason why many

What Makes a Good Storyline?

Like a novel you can't put down, there are certain elements to every enticing story. The most compelling brand stories should answer these three questions for people.

1. *What can you do for me?*

   People want to know first and foremost, in clear and certain terms, what problems you can solve for them. Successful brands that become indispensible to people always "own" several distinct buyer challenges and easily solve them. The most compelling stories create the link between obstacles and solutions, empathize with specific needs, and place their product or service as the "hero" in the story.

2. *Why are you different?*

   Telling people what makes your company different, not just better, than the competition will always keep them enthralled and delving deeper into your story. They want to know what your "secret sauce" is. Anyone can copy your product or service, but they can't copy the essence of who you are.

3. *Why should I stick around?*

   Take them on a journey. Once you've lured the reader into your story, you must make them want to finish and, better yet, greatly anticipate — and buy — the sequel. They may have bought into your brand and purchased your products or services, but you want them to covet the next big thing you offer.

companies in those industries come across as boring, impersonal, and pretty similar.

These business owners don't see their story as unique, interesting, or different. However, if that were the case, they wouldn't be in business very long ... or at all. The problem is not that they don't have a story; it's just that they don't understand what their story is or how they should be telling it.

Service industries and B2B companies must learn to change their thinking here and not talk to people so technically. Rather they should explain how they can solve problems and make people's lives easier, person-to-person, not "business to business." They need to see themselves as brands and create informational content with a distinct personality.

Here's an example of really bad website content from a B2B company:

> *(COMPANY) consistently exceeds its clients' expectations by providing extraordinary customer service and state of the art technology. Our carefully selected staff produces the highest quality (products) with the fastest turnaround.... We guarantee that your business will be attended to immediately with expertise and integrity.*

Can you even tell what type of business or industry this is about? Is it a law firm, IT company, business consultant, printing company? No clue, right? It's actually content from a court reporting firm. Why don't you know? Because the content tells no story and says nothing.

Whether you're a software developer, landscaping company, or auto parts manufacturer — you're a brand. If you're a doctor, architect, or accountant — you're a brand. If you run a pool store, hair salon, or dry cleaning business — you're a brand. Companies that don't think of themselves as a brand with a distinct reason for being, compelling points of difference, and an entity with a voice and personality, will never effectively tell their stories.

CASE STUDY

Pulling the Story from a B2B Brand

Think your business isn't that exciting? Paper converting likely doesn't sound thrilling either. But, here's an example of how Oren International, a paper converting company, transformed itself from boring and technical into an interesting and creative brand that stood out reams and reels from its stodgy competition.

Oren had a very outdated website, which did not communicate its full scope of services, or more importantly, what its employees are passionate about. It gave an overview of the company's basic products and services, but didn't even touch on the custom creative projects its team loved and wanted to focus more on.

The content was dry and offered factual information and industry terms. The Services page was basically a list of numbers, weights, and measurements for the types of paper Oren converts. Yawn.

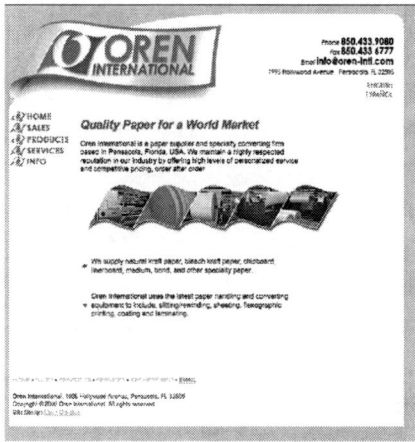

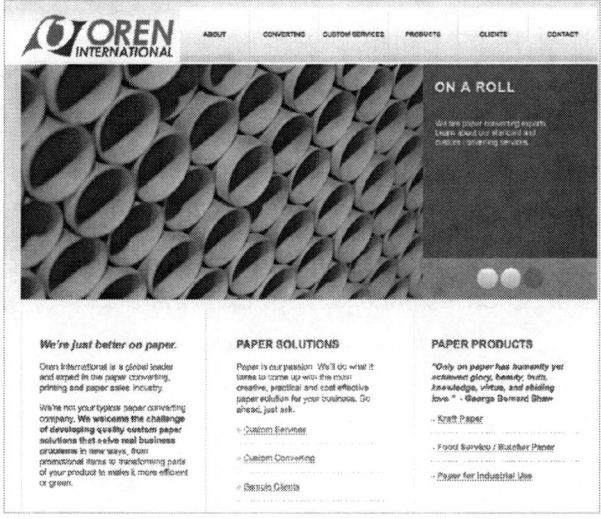

Oren International's homepage before (left) and after.

The content didn't tell the story of a fun, creative group with an amazing paper facility that services major clients — including restaurants, pharmaceutical companies, and advertising agencies — worldwide.

Once we got to know the real story behind its operations, we founds gems of information to bring out the team's personality and enhance its custom services through more fitting words and visuals. We learned about amazing branded paper solutions that Oren provides to restaurants, marketing companies, and even construction sites. We also saw the passion their people bring to the usage of paper. Oren is not your standard paper converter, but you would not have guessed that from the story (or lack thereof) this company was telling.

Oren's new content explains how the company partners with others to bring their visions to life and conveys enthusiasm for the possibilities of paper. It has a voice and perspective and effectively communicates what the company can do for clients — from developing innovative alternatives, to making them "greener," to collaborating with project engineers to execute ideas.

Within three months of the new site launch, Oren saw a 69 percent conversion rate for its e-book targeted at restaurants, and an 86 percent conversion rate for its e-book about the environment. Neither of these content pieces includes lists of measurements, weights, and numbers, but both show Oren's expertise and commitment to quality through interesting storytelling.

....

DO YOU HAVE AN AUTHENTIC BRAND STORY?

The real job of a brand story is to make emotional connections with people through authentic communication, transparency, interesting narrative, and bringing to light the brand's unique selling points that make it different from the competition. Making emotional connections is what top brand marketers do best, and those connections lead to greater loyalty … even "fan"atiscm.

Your brand's story has to resonate with people at a level that goes way beyond what's tangible (the functionality, features, and benefits of your products or services) to a personal place deep inside. You have to create something that they want to be a part of and show that you really "get" who they are and what they need.

When people really "get" your story, your brand has the potential to dominate a niche, transform an industry, and attract investors. Communicating the essence of your brand's big vision, and staying true to that in everything you do, is at the core of being a successful brand and staying on top of your industry. When people have a bond with your brand, they buy in; they're more likely to tell their friends, family, and social networks about who you are and what you do.

When customers and potential investors *don't* understand your story, ideas, products, or services, your business just blends into a sea of bland and boring companies. You may offer the greatest products and services in the world, but if you're not communicating that clearly through content with a distinct message, personality, and point of difference, no one will know. If your brand fails to connect with your audience and they aren't compelled to buy in, they surely won't be likely to buy at all. Just as in any good play — where a storyline needs to be strong before the director can hire actors and sell tickets — every brand should have its own plot and characters.

For example, Equal and Splenda are two brands in the same category, competing for an identical customer. These similarities make it even more important to create authentic brand stories to set their products apart. When Equal, the former alternative sweetener leader, was challenged by the launch of Splenda, its team made storytelling mistake number one — not telling one.

Equal, made with aspartame, positioned itself as a zero-calorie alternative to sugar and became a well-branded product known for its light blue packets. When Splenda launched onto the scene in sunny yellow packets, it quickly captured market share by introducing sucralose, a new zero-calorie sweetener "made from real sugar." According to *Businessweek*, by the late 2000s Splenda had overtaken Equal.[1]

Equal could have taken the success of Splenda to create a new product and storyline that spoke to its fans. Instead, Equal launched a similar product in the same yellow color package, without a story of its own. In fact, it was Splenda's story. Here is the copy from the Equal website:

> *"Equal Sucralose is the new, great tasting zero-calorie sweetener that's made with sucralose; the same sweetening ingredient used in Splenda No Calorie Sweetener but at a better value. Equal Sucralose is perfect for cooking and baking and can be used to replace sugar without compromising on taste."*

On the other hand, Splenda takes storytelling so seriously that an entire section of its website is dedicated to telling its brand story. Splenda doesn't assume brand loyalty will lure consumers; it gives consumers a brand story to be loyal to.

Telling your brand story (well) helps distinguish your company from the overload of information out there. It's why some brands, such as Apple and Starbucks, give people the warm fuzzies and create an irrational teenage-like crush in others.

A great example of two brands that are in the same category but that have two very different stories and voices are Method and Dawn. Here is descriptive content from each of their websites. Can you tell which story belongs to which brand?

Company 1
"Get more cleaning power. Get XXXX. It contains double the grease cleaning ingredients in every drop vs. the leading non-concentrated brand. XXXX has the power you need to fight tough grease and get the squeaky-clean dishes you're looking for. XXXX Antibacterial Hand Soap helps fight germs on hands when used as a hand soap."

Company 2
"No one sets out to neglect a cheesy casserole dish in the sink for days. But sometimes it happens. And when it does, you're glad that you have

an ultra grease-fighting and biodegradable dish soap to depend on. Especially since our natural dish liquid now comes in a new pump design, so you can squirt it directly into the sink or onto the sponge — or even directly on that cheese — with no drippy mess."

You're correct if you guessed that Company 1 is Dawn and Company 2 is Method. Dawn is a classic brand and has owned the message of grease fighting since the 70s. Method is a modern, vibrant, eco-friendly brand with a very distinct personality and voice that connects with its contemporary, style-driven customers. Neither is necessarily "better" than the other, but both speak directly to the type of consumer that uses its products.

MAKING EMOTIONAL CONNECTIONS

The emotion that a brand evokes in someone, or more importantly in a specific group of people, has a big impact on the brand's success or failure. Emotions play a huge role in how consumers act and react. Emotions drive decisions, prompt actions, and change mindsets, leading to strong loyalty and deep personal connections with certain brands. The heart of your consumer must connect with the soul of your brand. The level of this connection impacts the degree to which your audience and fans care about your brand, beyond its rational attributes.

This emotional connection is more psychological than logical and usually an unconscious feeling. Brands that develop distinct personas in people's minds project an image that people want to buy into. Someone may buy a product because it makes them feel smart, affluent, or sophisticated (e.g., "I'm really stylish and have good taste because I wear these shoes."). Generally, people buy products that are consistent with their positive, or aspirational, image of themselves.

One of the best-known books about the importance of emotional connections between consumers and brands is *Lovemarks: The Future Beyond Brands*.[2] Written in 2005 by Kevin Roberts, CEO Worldwide of Saatchi & Saatchi, the book tells the evolutionary story of how products, trademarks, and brands become "Lovemarks." Roberts says that by building respect and inspiring love, businesses can move the world. When brands make strong emotional connections with consumers, the feeling goes beyond brand loyalty and leaves an indelible mark that cannot be replaced. The Lovemarks theory:

> *"Lovemarks transcend brands. They deliver beyond your expectations of great performance. Like great brands, they sit on top of high levels of respect — but there the similarities end. Lovemarks reach your heart as well as your mind, creating an intimate, emotional connection that you just can't live without. Ever.*
>
> *"Take a brand away and people will find a replacement. Take a Lovemark away and people will protest its absence. Lovemarks are a relationship, not a mere transaction. You don't just buy Lovemarks, you embrace them passionately. That's why you never want to let go. Put simply, Lovemarks inspire Loyalty Beyond Reason."*

Brands We Absolutely Love…

We all have our Lovemarks. Here are a few examples of brands we cannot live without.

"I love J.Crew; I have since the late 80s when the company was mail-order only. I tore out the pages of the hot male models and hung them on my bedroom wall next to the current teen heartthrobs of the time. It wasn't just about the cute guys I dreamed of dating, it was the complete lifestyle depicted on the pages (tennis in Nantucket? Brunch in SoHo? Yes, please!). I also wanted to be the girls in the pictures and still try to emulate that perfectly preppy, intentionally disheveled but highly stylish look. I always joke that if money weren't an object I'd just order the entire J.Crew catalog every season and would be happy! Whenever I need a special occasion dress, a new bathing suit, or just feel like some retail therapy, J.Crew is still the first place I go. I just feel like everything they offer is "so me" and they've had my loyalty for 20 years. As a marketer and copywriter, I know it's the lifestyle story they created that I love just as much as the gorgeous nude sandals and pop-color tops. I not only love the clothes, but deeply admire their creativity, style, and whimsical language. The words on the pages (the puns, the alliteration!), in print and on the web, just sing to me, and each product description is like a mini short story, compelling me to covet each piece. Even the product names perfectly fit with the entire brand (Catie, Viv, Jules!), personified like the chic best friend you wish you had."

—*Debbie Williams*

"I'm not really a big shopper or brand addict. Nor do I have a great memory. So, it takes a lot for a company to gain my loyalty so that I'll love it so much that I choose its products or services over any other options. The company story that does it for me? LUNA. Lemon Zest, Blueberry Bliss, Iced Oatmeal Raisin ... I'll grab any of them off the shelf without even considering the "on sale" options nearby. LUNA had me at "hello" when I read their label years ago while scouring the gas station aisles for a healthy snack on my way to a camping trip. It was as if the words on the package were put there just for me at that exact moment in time: "Created by and for women, LUNA bars were the first bar just for us, with the vitamins and minerals our bodies need to stay healthy." Yay! From there, I couldn't stop learning more about the company. I love that the women at Clif Bar & Company took it upon themselves to create these delicious, nutritious snacks made just for other women (so the story goes). I love that the company cares about the environment, community, and their employees. I love that they've extended the brand to events like LUNAFEST, which features films about and for women, and

LUNA Chix for sports enthusiasts. Whenever I'm feeling like I need a little pick me up, not only does a LUNA bar satisfy my taste buds and growling stomach, but it also makes me feel connected to like-minded people and reminds me of the bigger world I live in. That's a story I don't want to live without."

—*Dechay Watts*

"Ralph Lauren has been my go-to brand for over 20 years. I am a regular wearer of bow ties and have always been inspired by the semi-formal look. I've always loved how Ralph Lauren told a consistent story through his catalog and stores. In most cases, it shows a lifestyle that I have always wanted to live outside of work. Ralph has a story for everyday life scenarios, out with friends or even traveling. But Ralph Lauren also offers the perfect fit for every occasion for those who work in the corporate world. Shopping in Ralph Lauren stores takes me on a journey of different emotions and sensory experiences, from the fine wood floors to sitting areas with leather sofas. Each area of the store is designed to fit a certain mood or occasion, always tying back to classic Americana. Ralph Lauren stores in Hong Kong are actually even better-looking than in other countries, including the U.S. I just love that feeling when you look straight forward as you walk into the store and see the iconic capsules of life on display. Ralph Lauren said, 'I don't sell fashion, I sell style.' And I love it." —*Said Baaghil*

With heightened market saturation and growing consumer apathy, it's more important than ever to connect honestly and intimately. Brands have to create long-term emotional relationships with consumers. Every company should know their customer, stay true to their mission, and be fearless about who they really are, because at the end of the day, you want to connect with real people … elicit an emotional reaction … make them feel happy, secure, or simply curious to learn more.

Chapter 1: Every Brand Has A Story...What's Yours?

HOW BRANDS ARE TELLING THEIR STORIES

Lay's Potato Chips

Frito Lay's went to great lengths in 2012 to transform the image of an "unhealthy" snack into something very positive with a focus on natural ingredients and honest information. Their website provided visitors with a Chip Tracker, which lets you enter your zip code and the product code from your bag of chips, to tell you where the potatoes were grown for that bag. There's also an interactive map showing you all of the farms in the U.S. where the potatoes for Lay's chips are grown. The site is filled with lots of other interesting content from recipes to information on sensible snacking and environmental causes. This is a great example of transparent storytelling done right.

Patagonia

Patagonia provides clothing and gear for camping and the outdoors. The company has earned great respect over the years for its genuine business practices and commitment to environmental integrity. Its straightforward company mission is to "build the best products and cause no unnecessary harm." To back up that

29

statement, Patagonia created the Footprint Chronicles. This cool interactive tool lets you track the environmental impact of a specific Patagonia product from its initial design to material sources through store delivery. It not only shows you where in the world the fabric and trim came from, but offers video interviews with people working in those countries who talk about the process from positives to challenges.

Origins

The beauty brand Origins is a prime example of a brand that is not afraid to live in a (very green) glass house and proudly show the world what it is all about. Origins is a brand built on authenticity. The company mission is to "create high-performance natural skincare that is powered by nature and proven by science." Origins' long-standing commitment to this philosophy has not wavered and is continually reaffirmed in every aspect of its brand story — from the products it creates to its website, recycled packaging, and business practices.

Origins is so transparent in its storytelling that it has a section in the main navigation of its website called Origins Story. In this area, Origins gladly opens its doors to share its Mission, Heritage, Products, Purity, Commitment, and Plant a Tree campaign. It reveals its company history, product ingredients, manufacturing processes, and dedication to environmental causes and issues. It also features more than a dozen videos with real customers talking about their skin transformations and the science behind the products.

Organic Valley

Organic Valley's mission is to "save family farms through agriculture." Its website features a tool called Find Your Farmer, which lets consumers virtually walk through the gates of the farms that produce the company's milk and other organic ingredients. Visitors can enter their zip code, find the Organic Valley farm closest to their home, and meet the actual farmers and their families. The site includes pictures and full profiles of every farmer that Organic Valley sources from and a directory of farms by region. The website also provides enticing content, including tips for health and nutrition and reasons for choosing organic.

The content you create is your stage, giving you a platform to share your expertise and knowledge with the world. It helps you become a resource that people will look to as a trusted authority and someone they want to do business with. Think about the ways you can share your story with the world.

SHEER ADVICE: HOW TO UNCOVER YOUR BRAND STORY

GET TO THE GUTS OF YOUR BRAND

No one can share their authentic brand story if they don't know what it is in the first place. You have to know who you are before you can explain who you are to someone else. Brands that don't have core value propositions in place have internal discrepancies about what they are even trying to say. You must be aligned internally and have a strong story in-house before you can share that story with the world. How can you have a conversation with someone if you don't even know what language you speak?

To tell your story, you have to know your reason for being in business and be able to articulate it clearly. What is your purpose? What is important to you? What makes your product different from the competition?

Business leaders must understand the essence of their own company's mission, and get real with themselves as to how durable and realistic that mission is. Businesses also must have a business plan and a clear corporate positioning, identifying who they are at the core, with a deep understanding of why they are in business and who they are in business for. The strategy, mission, and vision are part of the true essence of a brand story and all have to do with bringing the business' story in line with truth and reality. You can't build upon a weak foundation or there will always be cracks in your story.

Answering fundamental questions about why you're in business often reveals those vital nuggets of information about what makes you different, compelling, and interesting to others. Knowing where you've been will help you know where you're going.

DISCOVER YOUR "AHA!"

The main thing we do when working with clients at SPROUT Content is look for consistent and recurring themes in the answers they write down for us in our discovery questionnaire. We examine their comments compared to what they're currently saying publicly, and identify those vital special nuggets of information that make their story uniquely their own. There are often discrepancies in what people say within organizations and how they project those same ideas out to the world, so we create continuity in their message internally and externally. This helps create a consistent voice and tone and pinpoints the most unique defining characteristics to set a brand apart from the competition.

The important "aha" moments come when reviewing the answers, looking for trends, and finding those nuggets that resonate as something special. Answering questions helps you get words on paper so you can start to see your story unfold. Analyzing the answers uncovers exciting details that you may have been overlooking for years.

For example, we worked with a plastics company in Chicago that needed a website overhaul. The company site was basically a shell of information with canned content that had no personality or helpful information. When the owners submitted our questionnaire, it came back with one- or two-word answers and some factual dates about when the company started. As we reviewed their answers, the story of how the company was founded surfaced.

Not only was this company a plastics recycler, but also an industry pioneer. It emerged in Chicago in the 1960s as one of the first recycling companies in the country. This vital information was barely mentioned in the initial content discovery questionnaire because the owners didn't see it as an important detail. It was so ingrained in who they were as a company that they brushed it off as common sense. We used the information to craft key messages and content that brought their true story to life. Without going through the content questionnaire with the client, this important detail, the core of who this company is, would have gone undiscovered.

Here are a few basic questions to help you pull your story out of its box and begin a legacy of storytelling:

1. **What's your history?** From shampoo to chocolate or business logistics, people want to know the history of your products or services. Has anyone else owned your company? How did it come to be? Was there a creative, historical inspiration? Consider the example of Moleskine, the luxury notebook company, that created an historical fiction story around its notebooks ("the legendary notebook used by artists and thinkers over the past two centuries — among them Vincent van Gogh, Pablo Picasso, Ernest Hemingway, and Bruce Chatwin"). Now that's "creative" fiction, but chances are you actually have a solid story about your company's origins.

2. **Who are your main characters?** Whether people, places, or things, every brand story has main characters that helped the story take its shape. Were you inspired by a book? Was there a chance meeting with someone on a subway? Did you have an "aha" moment while jogging? Were you watching a James Bond movie when your light bulb went off? Did you discover an ingredient on a trip to India? Identify all of the people, real or fiction, and cast of characters that developed your story.

3. **What's your mission?** This is your ultimate *reason d'etre*. Why are you in business? What call are you responding to? What problems are you trying to solve? Method founders Eric Ryan and Adam Lowry set out to transform the consumer goods industry by creating products that "inspire a happy and healthy home revolution" with ingredients that "come from plants, not chemical plants." Method's annual revenue now exceeds $100 million.

4. **How have you failed?** Failure often breeds success. Showing people how you failed along the way and embracing those pitfalls transparently shows people that you're human, and will help them feel more connected to you on a personal level. Even Henry Ford failed in his early businesses and was broke five times before founding the Ford Motor Company.

> **Sometimes Less Isn't More**
>
> A client we worked with needed a complete content update to clearly show the extent of the products and services it offered. During the discovery Q&A, we learned that the company had begun as a family business decades before the date mentioned on its current website. Why would you shorten the time frame of your existence? Turns out, a younger generation had taken over, changed the name, and evolved the service offering. They went with an abridged timeline in an attempt to avoid confusion about the change in leadership. Their rich history was left in the dark ... and they weren't being completely honest about who they are (the people who had worked with them under the old ownership hadn't suddenly disappeared!).
>
> Today's customers are savvy. They can find information about your brand quickly and efficiently, whether you help them or not. If they start seeing mixed messages, they will quickly become skeptical and move on to another option.
>
> In this case, the entire story (told succinctly and well) painted a much more interesting picture of this company and created a huge point of differentiation from its competitors. Rather than hide the facts, it decided to come clean and capitalize on its legacy and deep knowledge base. It began to see improvements in its website traffic within the first month of rolling out its new brand image.

MIND THE GAPS

As you dive into thinking about these critical questions, pay attention to topics or subjects that you see people being hesitant to share. It's common practice to try to fill every month and year of your working life when creating a resume. You aren't "supposed" to have any gaps in your professional life. From our experience, however, the gaps often hold the key to why you have a story in the first place. Whether a year of work is missing from traveling the world, starting a family, or simply being unemployed, the best stories often come from those empty spaces.

A simple way to look for those intriguing gaps is to create a timeline for your company. Don't try to sugarcoat a slow year by blaming it on economic downturns or "transitions." Be honest with yourself and acknowledge the good and the bad. What you'll likely find is that during those times you normally wouldn't highlight, the most interesting part of your story will emerge.

A slow year may have forced your company to invent a new product or service. A rebranding campaign may have resulted from bringing on a new partner or letting someone go. The times where everything seemed status quo or even boring may have been when your next big idea was actually brewing underneath the surface. Whether you are a new or old brand, taking some time to remember why you started or how an idea came to you can be the essence of your story.

AUDIT YOUR CURRENT CONVERSATIONS

A thorough analysis of your current content assets (website, e-books, blog posts, videos, webinars, social media, etc.) is a great way to gain perspective on the story you are telling. It will gauge the effectiveness and consistency of your message and voice. Take a look at the information you are currently supplying and see if it's accurate. Literally read each page of your website, click on every link, and make notes of what stays, what goes, and what is needed. The same goes for your marketing materials and sales sheets. If you're not clearly explaining what you do, whom your products/services are for, and how you can help improve their lives or businesses, make note of that, too. This is the time to be true to yourself, so you can be authentic with your customers.

> ### A $3,000 Logo for a "Free" Homemade Website
>
> A doctor we know launched a private practice after moving back to his hometown. He had a great new office for which he spent thousands renovating and decorating. He also invested more than $3,000 on a new logo. Then he put this fancy new logo on a free, "homemade" WordPress template website.
>
> The website is not bad looking, but it fails to tell the story of the doctor's extensive volunteer work overseas, or his dramatic transformations of ill children and accident victims. Nor does it explain any of his service offerings beyond a long, non-bulleted list of words. If only our doctor friend had invested as much money, time, and resources into his content, perhaps more people would walk through the beautiful doors to see the lovely office and shiny new logo.

REMEMBER, WORDS MATTER

If you're selling a traditionally "boring" product or service (e.g., accounting or carpet cleaning), words can actually paint an exciting and interesting picture of your business and show how you will help or improve the lives of your customers. The right words can help you carve out a unique space and make memorable connections with people.

If you were stripped of your logo and your visual identity, your content should let people know who you are and what you are about. So many companies focus on the visual side of their story and neglect the importance of the words. They put all of their efforts into the look and design of a website, package, or product, without carving out a carefully crafted message that speaks to their audience. We've seen this too many times, especially when it comes to websites; businesses work with web developers to create a new site, but a lack of content holds up the entire process.

Your words and design must work as a cohesive and complete team to paint the full picture. Your package design, website, blog theme, catalog, or brochure might be drop-dead gorgeous, but if the words aren't compelling, no one will keep reading. Or even worse, your words might be brilliant and captivating, but if the design doesn't draw people in, you're done.

> **The Power of the Right Words**
>
> Words stir the imagination, spark emotion, and transport people into a different mindset. A great example of this transformation is seen in a video that went viral in 2011 called "The Power of Words." It depicts a blind, homeless man sitting on a city street collecting change. The sign initially in front of him read simply, "I'm blind, please help." Most people just walk by, with the occasional passerby dropping some change. A woman walking by stopped and rewrote his sign to say, "It's a beautiful day and I can't see it." Wow! Why do these new words become impossible to ignore? They forge an emotional connection between the experience of one person and another. They make the passersby relate in an entirely different way to what and whom they see. This short film illustrates how the power of words can dramatically change your message and effect upon the world. Brands should do the same.

Brand stories are far more than a catchy slogan or tagline. Brand stories offer a perspective and share a philosophy through words on websites, social media, packaging, videos, and more. Imagine if you were looking for a new face cream and found dozens of packages with only colors and pictures and no description of the product benefits, ingredients, or promised results? What if you were searching the Internet to find a new camera and just found pictures of cameras, with no information on features or product reviews? Words matter, and brands that tell their stories, not just show them, have a huge competitive advantage.

CLEAR CONCLUSION

You have to know who you are before you can explain who you are to someone else. Be sure you have a value proposition in place and that everyone on your team is on the same page. Reflect upon where you came from, what makes you different, and how you're going to share your story with the world. Dig in and really figure out what factors will make an emotional connection with your audience — then go out and shout your story from the rooftops!

CHAPTER 2
Give Away Your Knowledge: Be Transparent to Build Trust

People researched and digested 10.4 unique pieces of content before making a purchasing decision.[1]
—Jim Lecinski
Google's Winning the Zero Moment of Truth 2011 ebook

Today, more than ever, brands have a tremendous opportunity to gain loyal customers by creating original, authentic content and sharing their expertise. Think about it. Why do you consistently buy one brand or call one service company over another? Standing out in the crowd of noise by truly being helpful and real can be done — and easily, if done right. The pioneers of content innovation through brand storytelling understood this, years before content marketing was an actual industry. They had the foresight to see that delivering helpful information to their audience in a new way would build trust and loyalty, leading to long-term relationships, some of which still carry on today. Consider the following:

- Harley Davidson's *The Enthusiast* was first published by the motorcycle legend in 1916 and is still the longest-running motorcycle publication in the world.

- Dutch Boy's *The Painter* was launched in 1942 and featured articles like "Saving Leftover Paint" and "Mixing 20-Gallon Batches of White Lead Paint." The painting pub was sent for free to painters and paint dealers.

- The 1940s saw publications such as Merck & Co.'s *The Merck Review*, *New York Life Insurance Company Review*, and *The DuPont Magazine*.

- The first branded content is widely credited as tractor company John Deere's *The Furrow*. Published in 1895, this was, and still is, a consumer magazine. *The Furrow* is not filled with canned marketing messages, but valuable information to help farmers be more successful. Today, the publication has more than 1.5 million readers in 40 countries and is published in 12 languages.

This early-era branded content exemplifies the visionary ideas these leaders had for creating and sharing "free" content that helped educate their audiences, tell their stories, and make real connections with their customers. Imagine what these ingenious innovators would have done with tools such as the Internet, email, and social media channels. Armed with modern tools and technologies, brands have limitless opportunities for taking their stories to new places, through new mediums, to reach an audience ... sometimes within seconds.

CONNECTING THROUGH CONTENT MARKETING

Once upon a time, not so long ago, marketers spun messages to match consumers' fairy-tale dreams. Now, we live in a time where people expect products and services to deliver on promise. Technology is connecting us, creating a sense of oneness that gives people real decision-making power. We are a consumer army, equipped with immediate electronic response tools such as social media and blogs, where complete transparency is not only expected, but also utterly essential to a brand's success.

Content marketing has emerged as one of the best ways for brands to connect with consumers while maintaining their integrity and authenticity. In fact, the nature of content marketing is to connect directly to consumers through honest, relevant, interesting communication.

Every business in the world has the opportunity to get in on the act — to be a publisher of information. Content enables you to share tried-and-true experience, and, if done right, can ultimately position you as the leader in your industry. Once you are known as an expert in your market, it will be difficult, if not impossible, for any other company to come in between you and your loyal fan base.

> *"Content marketing is the practice of creating relevant and compelling content in a consistent fashion to a targeted buyer, focusing on all stages of the buying process, from brand awareness through to brand evangelism."*
> *—Joe Pulizzi, Founder, Content Marketing Institute*

Content marketing is:

- Creating an interesting and compelling story, telling it well, and participating in the ongoing conversation
- Attracting, engaging, and acquiring an audience by providing valuable content (information)
- NOT ... spinning a message, interrupting, or delivering information "with a catch."

By providing valuable content that helps people find solutions and answers, you capture their interest. By capturing their interest, you gain their trust and eventually their loyalty to your product or service. Brands should explore opportunities to tell true stories in creative ways that will allow them to continually connect with their audience and grow those relationships.

HOW BRANDS ARE GIVING AWAY KNOWLEDGE

Ever since "Content is King" became the most overused buzz phrase of the decade, many companies have made the mistake of trying to churn out as much content as possible, often with disregard to how original, strategic, or useful it really is to their audience. We've all been victims of boring, generic content, canned newsletters, and blog posts stuffed with over-used industry jargon that have left us numb.

That said, there are plenty of good examples of brands giving away their knowledge in creative ways to connect with their audiences. Here are a few examples.

Sherwin-Williams STIR

SwStir.com is an online magazine from Sherwin-Williams that offers great tips from a team of color experts including an architect, interior designer, and the brand's director of color marketing. STIR is a virtual encyclopedia of color, educating people on various color histories and their significance. It explains how to make your home "green," and educates through videos featuring artists and designers.

It is obvious that STIR is a Sherwin-Williams site, but there is no direct sell, opportunity to purchase a product, discounts, or offers. It's a site that's a story in itself, passionate about the exploration of color and design and inspiring people to see "color in a new light." The company is also transparent in its mission for STIR, which is posted right on the website: "Sherwin-Williams has always been committed to serving as your strategic design partner. Through STIR, we're dedicated to providing you with a valuable resource that you look forward to receiving, reading, and exploring."

Colgate-Palmolive

Colgate-Palmolive's home page states, "Every day, millions of people like you trust our products to care for themselves and the ones they love." The CEO's message begins with, "The small soap and candle business that began in New York City early in the 19th century is now serving hundreds of millions of consumers worldwide." Colgate-Palmolive tells stories through facts and figures that remind its consumers of its trustworthiness. To spread this story even further, Colgate-Palmolive created an online Oral and Dental Health Resource Center with videos, interactive guides, and more than 400 articles that provide valuable information to consumers.

McDonald's Canada

McDonald's Canada encourages consumers to ask ANY, yes any, question on its website (Yourquestions.mcdonalds.ca), which staff personally answers. From "How is it that a McDonald's burger does not rot?" to "Do you use kangaroo meat in your food?"… the McDonald's Canada content is as authentic as it gets.

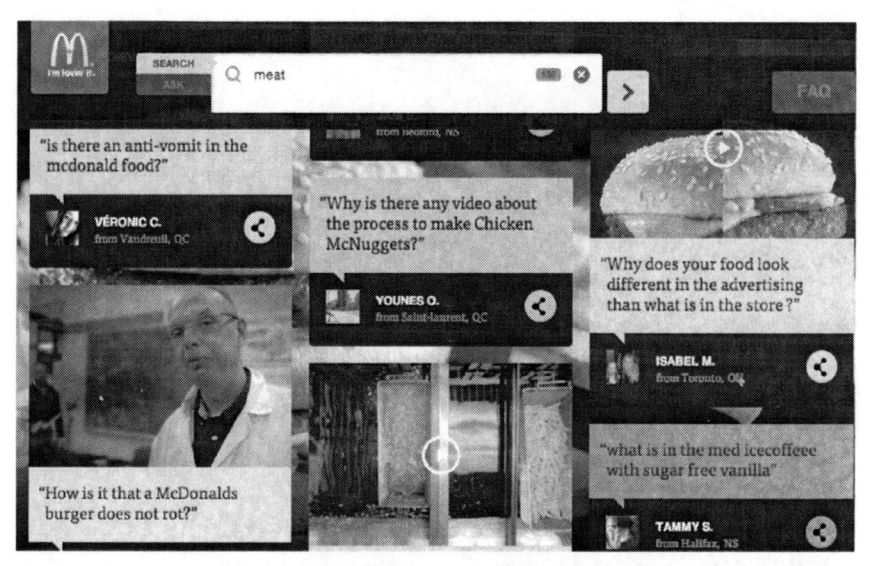

McDonald's Canada encourages consumers to ask questions on its website (Yourquestions.mcdonalds.ca).

General Electric

One of the ways that GE stays interesting and relevant to consumers is through its Ecomagination website. Ecomagination is a forum for fresh thinking and conversation about clean technology and sustainable infrastructure. The site is set up as a magazine with an experienced managing editor, editor-at-large, and editorial staff of writers and journalists. A key metric used to determine the success of this storytelling initiative is the act of sharing.

"At the end of the day, if the content isn't good enough for the end user to want to share it with a friend or colleague, we haven't quite succeeded," says Katrina Craigwell, digital marketing manager at GE.[2]

JetBlue

JetBlue's blog, Blue Tales, literally opens the cockpit doors to reveal "A Day in the Life" of its employees. The blog's "Unpacked" series demystifies hot topics in the airline industry, from what really happens to your bag to how they prepare for weather emergencies. The brand has more than 1.6 million followers on Twitter (more than any other airline) and is not afraid to shout out tips and share knowledge from 100,000 feet and beyond.

We are pretty wowed at how honest and real many brands are being. True transparency not only builds trust, but also raises the bar for other companies to follow.

> *"Transparency is not a choice. It's going to happen. The only choice is does it happen to you or do you participate in it? When it happens to you it's proven to be really ugly."*
> —Alex Bogusky, Founder, COMMON

EVERYONE CAN PLAY

Megabrands aren't the only ones with the opportunity to give away valuable knowledge and be honest in what they reveal. Any size business can write a blog, interact with customers through social media, create videos, and design infographics to share their expertise.

Content levels the playing field. Sometimes, small- and medium-sized businesses do a better job at sharing interesting, original information than do big corporations. They don't have as many layers to go through to create and approve content, and thus their content can be published faster and is often more genuine in tone and sentiment. Small businesses can even beat big companies to the chase when launching technologies and innovations, announcing breaking news, or being the first to do something in their industry. Here are a few examples.

The Old World Napa Inn

The owners of the Old World Napa Inn have mastered the art of creating genuine helpful content to assist travelers. They freely give away their knowledge to help people make travel plans, regardless of whether people choose their Inn or not. Planners visiting TripAdvisor can find delightfully detailed answers from the Innkeepers themselves in the Reader Forums. The staff answers questions regarding best time of year to visit Napa Valley, complete with weather forecasts, and

Chapter 2: Give Away Your Knowledge: Be Transparent to Build Trust

> **FAQ: Best time of year to visit Wine Country? Weather???**
> Aug 02, 2007, 3:06 PM
>
> Napa_Old_World_Inn
> Napa, CA
>
> Destination Expert
> for Napa Valley
>
> posts: 4,743
> reviews: 2
>
> 🔖 Save this Post
>
> The wine country is beautiful almost any time of year.
>
> It's quite slow from Jan 2 through most of March, with the exception of Valentine's Day and Columbus Day weekend, when the valley is packed to capacity.
>
> Jan 2 through March is a favorite time of year for many repeat visitors-- it's when we have the Mustard Festival, with vibrant wild mustard blossoms growing in rows between the bare grape vines.
>
> This time of year is a "best kept secret" for many folks who come to the wine country every year for a visit-- things are slower, so they can linger at tasting rooms and learn more about each winery, restaurants have open tables, so they can enjoy their favorite spots, and both airfare and room rates are very low, meaning many people choose to stay here for a week instead of just a day or two. This is our favorite time of year, since we get a chance to visit with some of our guests a bit more (since they stay longer).

By freely sharing their knowledge, the Old World Napa Inn has become a trusted resource for people looking to visit the Napa Valley area.

details about the grape harvesting seasons. The Innkeepers also provide "best kept secrets" so travelers get the most accurate inside scoop on Napa that doesn't come in most generic travel guides.

This valuable information lends a sense of credibility, showing that the Innkeepers are experts on insider Napa knowledge and will take the time to offer helpful guidance to visitors planning activities. In addition, they have excellent content on their website and blog and post lots of authentic traveler reviews.

CorePower Yoga

Denver-based CorePower Yoga uses social networks as outlets to build relationships and awareness about yoga. Its #HelpfulYogi is an online conversation where users submit questions via Facebook and Twitter, which are answered by yoga instructors. Engaging its audience is working; CorePower Yoga is now the nation's largest yoga chain in a field that has been dominated by mom-and-pop companies. Its growth plan is rooted in branding and digital marketing, forgoing TV and print ads for word-of-mouth recommendations and a consistent customer experience across its many locations. Online videos provide customers the option to experience a yoga class anytime and anywhere … at least until there's a CorePower Yoga on your corner.

Independent beauty boutiques, chocolate companies, court reporters, fashion designers, and trucking companies are now equipped with the same tools as global corporations for creating content that connects with real people who need and want their products. The key is giving away helpful information that showcases your knowledge so your audience perceives you as a trusted authority and someone they want to do business with.

CAN YOU GIVE AWAY TOO MUCH?

We don't think so, but the fear of "oversharing" is a common concern, especially among small and midsize businesses new to embracing the transparency required in marketing today.

The Sales Lion

Marcus Sheridan, author of The Sales Lion blog, built his entire business around sharing too much. During the economic downturn in 2008, Marcus knew he had to do something different to generate leads online for his fiberglass pool business, River Pools and Spas in rural Virginia. His search led him to HubSpot and the concept of inbound marketing, which he dove into enthusiastically and educated himself about to invigorate his sales. As Marcus started using HubSpot's inbound marketing tools and content management system, he felt empowered to develop valuable content that would help his customers, even the ones he hadn't met yet. Without any prior experience, he took control of his content and began to share his knowledge in a blog.

According to Marcus, "If your customers have questions, it's your duty to answer them … with utter transparency. Why not be brutally transparent with your approach to business? Why not be the voice of your industry? Why not address issues that no one else has the bravery or guts to talk about? And why not earn the trust of all those around you in the process?"

Marcus created a list of the top questions he received over the years and wrote his first blog post answering the number one question, "What are the problems with fiberglass pools?" He continued this process to write more than 400 blog posts, being brutally honest and providing information that competitors and his industry tried to hide. He told people why fiberglass pools might not be right for them and even revealed "secret" information on the manufacturing process. For example, competitors never published information regarding pricing for others to see, but River Pools and Spas published market prices of pool material on its blog. A post titled "Fiberglass Pool Prices: How Much is My Pool Really Going to Cost?" received 20,359 page views and 84 inbound links.

Within a year, Marcus increased his website traffic from 176 organic searches per month to more than 6,900 visits per month, increasing website traffic by 300 percent. Now, River Pools and Spas is the most popular blog in the pool industry and the number one pool company in the U.S. specializing in fiberglass pools.

Why was Marcus so successful? **Because he answered questions publicly that competitors were afraid to talk about.**

We often work with clients who are fearful of revealing too much. When we suggest blog post topics that go more in-depth about custom services, some company founders balk at the idea for fear of "giving away their secrets" to competitors. They don't want to spawn ideas for competitors to learn about their concepts and take away clients.

What these business owners don't understand is that the opposite is true. The big winners in storytelling create memorable moments between their brand and their audience. It's been proven time and time again. Brands that formulate and capitalize upon a unique perspective in their industry nab a leadership position. When you take a stance and have a thought-provoking point-of-view, it inspires people to buy into your brand story before they even buy your product or service — especially if you're one of the only companies in your industry creating original content and educating people about a service industry most people know nothing about.

Take a lesson from Marcus; he was not only a content pioneer in his market, he also became a dominant ruler in his field. There's no reason why you can't, too.

SHEER ADVICE: HOW TO GIVE AWAY YOUR KNOWLEDGE

You don't have to be in the "big leagues" to reach a vast audience and build real relationships. While it takes resources, organizational support, and talent to get the job done right, content is your company's stage. Marketers and small business owners can write blogs, interact with customers through social media, share presentations, and even create videos. Each published piece serves as a platform to share expertise and knowledge with the world.

SPEAK THROUGH YOUR WEBSITE

When searching for a company online, whether a doctor, hair salon, or gym, people want to find details to help them make informed decisions. They want to find the who, what, and why from the content you provide. Your website content is your personal greeting to potential or existing customers. It's your introduction; your opportunity to connect one-on-one; your 24/7 sales team that works while you're busy doing other things, or sleeping.

When you call someone and get an automated voice message, it feels impersonal doesn't it? The same is certainly true with your website content. No one relates to cookie cutter, unoriginal messages. Showcase your knowledge through custom, compelling content to set your brand apart from the competition and make a memorable impression. Your content can foster a connection from the start.

As Jesse James Garrett says in his book, *The Elements of User Experience:* "The single most important thing websites can offer to their users is content that those users will find valuable."[3] Valuable translates into:

- Information that **connects to users**
- Links that **keep users engaged**
- A voice that **users remember.**

DITCH THE JARGON

No one wants to go to a company website and read a bunch of tedious industry jargon or buzzwords about "bottom lines" and "optimal performance." They want to know what your business can do for their business, or how your product or service can actually improve their lives in some way. There is nothing worse than visiting a company site with clip art and lots of nonsense phrases that tout their products as "innovative," "new," or "the best." Blah, blah, blah. No one cares!

In his book, *Speak Human*, Eric Karjaluoto says:

> *"In your gut you know that most marketing is a load of crap. It's vague, inhuman, and backed by nonsense that seems designed to bamboozle. It is about exaggerating wildly and telling lies. Take a walk through any shopping mall and look at the messages found in promotional materials. The first thing you'll notice is that they're founded on hyperbole."*[4]

While creative narrative is fine, particularly for more luxurious industries like fashion and beauty that are selling an image and aspiration, complete exaggeration to the point of lies is sadly commonplace in the marketing world. Many businesses are so busy focused on one-upping each other, that they've lost sight of who they are and that they are people, ultimately in business to help other people. Speak to those people as if you're a person, too.

BE A GIVER

Your website should not only offer good content, but also inspiring calls-to-action that lead to free incentives (e.g., e-books that can be downloaded for additional, helpful information). When people are inspired to take action on your site and fill out a form to receive valuable content, you can start to form an honest relationship and start capturing qualified leads. They are telling you that they like what they see and want to know more about you.

Here are a few ways that you can share helpful information with people that will let your expertise shine, without just "selling" to them.

- **Create a "resources" e-book** answering frequently asked questions about your business or service. Include a handy reference guide of blogs, media outlets, brands, and experts in different categories that you would suggest turning to for ideas and knowledge.

- **Share quotes from your favorite industry experts** or authors, celebrities, historical figures, and cultural icons. Also keep a list of favorite one-liner gems from conferences, workshops, and seminars you attend.

- **Review a product**, service, or book that other people in your community or industry will care about. Look at helpful tools you use or ones you've wanted to check out. You'll kill two birds with one stone, learning something new and creating helpful content.

- **Create a blog.** Blogs are a great way to share your expertise and educate consumers with the added benefit of driving traffic leads. In fact, 79 percent of companies that have a blog reported a positive ROI for inbound compared to just 20 percent of companies who do not have a blog, according to HubSpot's *2013 State of Inbound Marketing Report.* The report also says 82 percent of marketers who blog daily acquire a customer using their blog, as opposed to 57 percent of marketers who blog monthly.[5] A blog is one of the greatest resources that businesses have to answer their customers' questions, show they are listening, and shine a bright light on their vast industry knowledge.

Being a giver of helpful insider information will position you as a beneficial resource that people will remember, connect with, and come back to again and again. Don't create fictional stories, but share what's real. Remember, it's better to give than receive, and in business, if you give, people usually reciprocate with their business and loyalty.

Finding Inspiration for Your Blog

Every once in a while we all find ourselves in dry spell. The good news is that inspiration can come in many forms, if you know where to look. Here are a few simple ways to get those creative juices flowing again and help keep your blog interesting, original, and authentic.

- **Write a curated blog post** of the most interesting industry news you read each week. You're reading it anyway, so make the most of your time and share it with your community. Write a quick summary of the top five stories you read (that's just once a day!) and include a link to the story. Chances are, your followers will be interested, too.

- **Ask your clients** or other community peers if they would like to write a guest blog post or send in a video testimonial. Great content doesn't have to come from you directly. There are lots of other resources and industry experts you can tap into. You may not like being in front of the camera, but a lot of people do.

- **Scan the headlines.** Check out current news for the latest scoop on industry trends, stats, studies, new products, technologies, or other topics related to your business. Simply set up Google Alerts and RSS feeds of your favorite industry and other news sources and have the headlines sent right to your email inbox. Then scan the headlines for the most interesting topics each day and start filling in a blog editorial calendar with post ideas.

- **Look at your emails and blog comments.** Your own email inbox and comments on blog posts can spark great ideas for blog posts. What questions are your customers, clients, and audience asking the most? What topics have you recently discussed with colleagues? It's very likely that if one person wants to know more about a topic, others will, too.

CLEAR CONCLUSION

Some companies focus on creating relevant, valuable, and helpful information, passionately telling their story with the world; however, many others are just churning out noise as fast as they can. Don't be one of those companies.

Be honest in the information you share, lose your fear of being too transparent, and recognize opportunities to educate your audience. Empowering your audience through helpful content will help you build trust and create more authentic and lasting relationships with the people you want to reach. In turn, those people will reward you with their business.

CHAPTER 3
Be Consistent:
Tell the Same Story Across All Channels

"Companies are becoming more and more transparent whether they like it or not. The lag time between brand and culture is becoming less and less, which is really scary for companies where the brand they are trying to portray is different from their internal culture."
—Tony Hsieh, CEO, Zappos, in "The Naked Brand"[1]

If you spoke in a different tone of voice every time you met someone, they would probably think you were crazy. The same goes for your business: **We're funny … no, we're serious … no wait, we're sarcastic and silly!**

Inconsistency in tone, voice, and message makes you look like a brand with multiple personality disorder. Having a consistent voice and perspective, across all channels, inside and outside of your company, will make a memorable connection with people and make your company one that people trust.

Brand stories can be told in many different forms with an evolving story line and cast of characters, but must be consistent, avoiding any holes. From your in-house culture to every touch point with customers, your authentic brand story must trickle down throughout every interaction you have with the world. It should shine through in all the content you create and all of your marketing efforts —from your website to emails, social media, videos, packaging, and even your customer service conversations. Consistently telling your story across all channels helps people determine whether they want to let you into their lives and their wallets.

Do you know that it takes six to seven brand impressions for someone to remember your company? Every single impression you make is important, from the first one on. The more consistent you are each time you tell your story, the more memorable the imprint will be.

Many brands get trapped in a minefield of inconsistency across different channels because they don't take the time to plan from the start. Then, they blame lack of budget and resources as the reason, and the mess never gets fixed. But at least they have a website, right? Not true. Being inconsistent from channel to channel will only confuse people and you will certainly need to surpass six or seven impressions to make an indelible mark.

CONSISTENCY FROM THE INSIDE OUT

Your story must be told the same way, from the inside out. From internal communications, to how your office looks and how people answer the phone, keeping your story consistent from the mailroom to the boardroom is fundamental to maintaining authenticity.

Imagine if the entire staff at the corporate offices of Sephora wore no makeup at all, or if the headquarters of Pottery Barn looked like a cold gray warehouse filled with cardboard boxes? Or, what if you called Apple for tech support and spoke to someone who was un-savvy, long-winded, and complicated? Your team has to share your passion and fully understand your brand story in order to tell your story consistently.

Zappos

Zappos is a good example of a company that lives and breathes its brand story consistently from its employees to its online retail experience. The company culture is based around the philosophy that happy employees lead to loyal employees and happy customers lead to loyal customers. A focus on happiness shines through all of the brand's interactions.

The Zappos headquarters in Las Vegas is comparable to Disney, one of the happiest places on Earth. The company has a quirky and whimsical corporate culture and throws lots of parties. It also pays for health insurance and has a life coach on staff. This culture of happiness makes people want to work at Zappos. According the film *The Naked Brand*, the company received 20,000 applications for 250 job openings in 2010, which makes Zappos more selective than Harvard.[2]

Because employees personally feel CEO Tony Hsieh's dedication to happiness, they express a good attitude outward to the company's customer base. Zappos is synonymous with great customer service. Instead of spending millions on marketing and advertising, Zappos invests in the highest level of customer service possible, offering a 24/7 call center with real people, a 365-day return policy, and free, two-way shipping.

When they do spend money on advertising, they keep it real and authentic to the brand culture. In 2010, Zappos launched an ad campaign with puppets reenacting real customer service calls. The customer service reps helped everyone from a woman trying to find a mystery man who sent her a dress, to a woman who was "emotionally unprepared" to get a dress the day after she ordered it. Zappos sometimes sends orders overnight just to charm customers. In this case, the customer received the dress so quickly that she wanted to send it back. In most cases, this generous and unexpected act results in repeat buyers, which is how the company has grown its brand (in 2005, Zappos reported that 60 percent of all of its sales were to repeat buyers[3]).

Creating consistent, positive experiences — both inside and out — has grown Zappos into a place where people want to work, a brand that people choose to talk about, and an online store that customers repeatedly shop from.

Target

Target is another one of our favorite examples of consistency across the board. By now, you probably recognize the adorable puppies, whimsical red products, and vibrant bulls-eye a mile away. Target employees seem to bounce around the store in their red shirts, asking if you need anything, opening up registers when lines get long, and treating customers as "guests."

Thanks to hip campaigns, stylish in-store displays, and collaborations with high-end designers who create limited-edition goods that often sell out in minutes, people often forget that Target is a discount store (it is?!). People respond to the consistently fun, friendly, helpful, and fashionable vibe that Target has established, even referring to the retailer as "Targét," as if it were a chic French design house. Target's public persona often belies its mass-market status.

Target stays consistent with its brand story — from its brick-and-mortar stores to its online store, product offerings, and employee communications — creating a trusting connection with consumers.

THE CONTENT LIFECYCLE

If your brand story isn't consistent throughout the entire content lifecycle, it will certainly have flaws and lose people along the journey. Let's look at an example of all the touch points where a brand has the opportunity to consistently tell the same story – from package copy, to sales collateral, to online content.

Say a hair care company launches a new product. The information on the product packaging can be used as the basis for an in-store brochure and sales collateral. That new product also can be featured on a web page on the brand's site, along with descriptive content that educates consumers about what the product will do for their hair. Then, a press release can be written announcing the product launch. The release should include keywords with links back to the product page on the website.

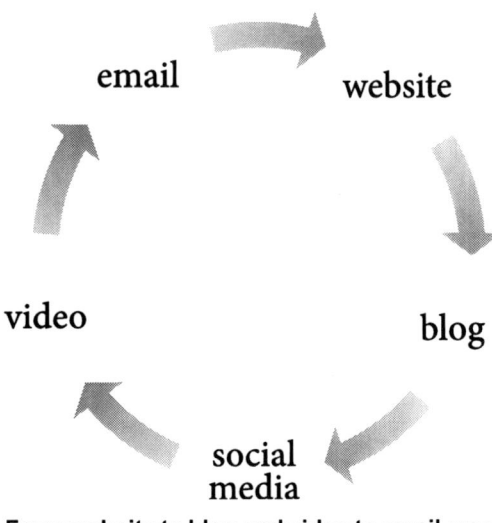

From website to blog and video to email, your brand story should be told consistently throughout the content lifecycle.

The brand manager can then write a blog post announcing the new product, describing all the great benefits it offers. Next, the team can send out an email to subscribers, using the same key messages, to issue a coupon code for purchase of the product. Finally, the team can craft a series of relevant posts for all of the brand's social media outlets, reinforcing the key messages and linking to the website. Ta-da! Done right, the brand has created an effective content storytelling lifecycle.

> **Maximize the Impact of Your Content**
>
> Remember, not all customers are connected to a brand in the same way. They can choose to receive information at one or a variety of content touch points. If you publish a great blog post, it doesn't mean that your Facebook fans saw it, your Twitter followers read it, or your email newsletter subscribers noticed it.
>
> Companies should invest the time and resources to develop several solid pieces of content and recycle them to get the most leverage out of them. For example, after putting together a presentation, write a blog post highlighting the key messages, and post the presentation on SlideShare. The post and presentation also can increase SEO and come up in relevant searches on the topic or your name or industry. If you write an informative e-book, break it out into a series of blog posts and share them through social media channels. A single piece of content should never be just that.

BRANDS THAT ARE CONSISTENTLY HITTING THE MARK

Here are just a few great examples of fearless companies that are consistently and compellingly capturing the attention of their audience seamlessly and transparently throughout their content lifecycle.

Chipotle

Chipotle Mexican Grill consistently shares its story with the world across all touch points. You can see the content lifecycle begin on its website where *Chipotle Story* is a main navigation button. The button takes you to a video and open letter from founder Steve Ells about how the company started and its commitment to sustainable, compassionate farming and the environment.

The story continues with branded content in an online magazine called *The Chipotle Cultivate Foundation*. The website includes educational information about sustainable farming, animal welfare, and environmental impact, with messaging that ties into Chipotle's core philosophies.

Another content piece that keeps the story alive is Chipotle's "Back to the Start" video, which features a haunting rendition of Coldplay's "The Scientist," performed by Willie Nelson. The short animated film depicts the life of a farmer as he slowly transforms his family farm into an industrial animal factory before realizing the error of his ways. The viewer is taken on a journey to see the farm reborn into what Chipotle believes a farm is intended to be, where animals are free to wander the earth and green grass grows. The film and soundtrack were commissioned by Chipotle to raise awareness of the importance of developing a sustainable food system, and at least 70 percent of the proceeds from the song sales on iTunes benefit the Foundation.

"Back to the Start" won the first-ever branded content Cannes Lions Grand Prix at the Cannes Film Festival in 2012. An article in *Ad Age* cited Jury President Avi Savar, founder and chief creative officer of Big Fuel, as saying, "What tipped the balance in favor of Chipotle was the way content lived across multiple touch points, and built one voice across all those touch points."[4]

Grape-Nuts

Post Foods' Grape-Nuts cereal has been around as a healthy and natural food source since 1879, before the current trend toward healthy living began. In an authentic and educational way, Grape-Nuts ties its long history and dedication to healthy living into a motivational crusade across all communication points.

Grape-Nuts recently adopted the theme "What's Your Mountain?"

to encourage consumers to tackle challenges by staying healthy and true to themselves. The Grape-Nuts website says, "Whether you're pushing through a tough workout, or simply trying to create a wholesome and healthy lifestyle, the natural whole-grain goodness of Grape-Nuts packs the power to help you climb your personal mountain."[5]

This message also appears in television commercials showing historic videos of famous athletes achieving their goals with the help of Grape-Nuts. The Grape-Nuts Facebook page keeps the theme going by asking, "What mountain are you conquering today?"

In addition, Grape-Nuts sponsors inspirational videos and articles on Patch.com to showcase people striving for positive change and healthy lifestyles. The message of staying healthy and motivated is even carried offline to special events, such as one that was held in Manhattan, featuring a 30-foot rock wall that people could climb and attach a pennant to stating, "What's Your Mountain?"[6]

Holstee

Holstee is an ecommerce marketplace for sustainable goods "designed with a conscience." The brand started small, creating only T-shirts with a holster for a phone. Holster + tee = Holstee. The company started as a side project for three friends who wanted to create a better type of business based on their shared passion for living a meaningful life. Before launching any products, the trio created a brand manifesto that captured the essence of their company mission.

After enduring the manufacturing process, Co-Founder Fabian Pfortmüller and the rest of the team realized that their conscientious concept had potential to transform the retail industry.

In an article in Mashable, Fabian said, "We believe that people are hungry to know: Where's a product from? Where is it made? Why does it matter for me to buy the product?"[7] Based on this philosophy, Holstee expanded its offering from T-shirts to selling a range of sustainable and upcycled goods. The brand's founders have established strong consumer demand by creating a lifestyle and living out their manifesto in all that they do, not basing success purely on revenue.

Their candor and honesty set the foundation for their entire story, which they live out every day. On Black Friday in 2012, Holstee showed that their beliefs matter more than profits when they shut down their website on the biggest shopping day of the year, leaving only a note inspiring people to spend time with family and friends, not money on products they likely don't essentially need.

The Holstee manifesto is on the brand's website, has been broken into video segments, and ignited a Re-Pin craze on Pinterest. The team's blog speaks to humanitarian issues, and its MyLife online community showcases stories from people who have embraced the manifesto and how it inspired them to transform their own lives. The Holstee Fellowship gives away $1,000/month to people looking to follow their own dream … just like the founders did in 2009.

Holstee represents a blend of ethos and sustainability, designing, and curating with a conscience. The company was founded on a mission before a product was developed.

THIS IS YOUR LIFE. DO WHAT YOU LOVE, AND DO IT OFTEN. IF YOU DON'T LIKE SOMETHING, CHANGE IT. IF YOU DON'T LIKE YOUR JOB, QUIT. IF YOU DON'T HAVE ENOUGH TIME, STOP WATCHING TV. IF YOU ARE LOOKING FOR THE LOVE OF YOUR LIFE, STOP; THEY WILL BE WAITING FOR YOU WHEN YOU START DOING THINGS YOU LOVE. STOP OVER ANALYZING, ALL EMOTIONS ARE BEAUTIFUL. LIFE IS SIMPLE. WHEN YOU EAT, APPRECIATE EVERY LAST BITE. OPEN YOUR MIND, ARMS, AND HEART TO NEW THINGS AND PEOPLE, WE ARE UNITED IN OUR DIFFERENCES. ASK THE NEXT PERSON YOU SEE WHAT THEIR PASSION IS, AND SHARE YOUR INSPIRING DREAM WITH THEM. TRAVEL OFTEN; GETTING LOST WILL HELP YOU FIND YOURSELF. SOME OPPORTUNITIES ONLY COME ONCE, SEIZE THEM. LIFE IS ABOUT THE PEOPLE YOU MEET, AND THE THINGS YOU CREATE WITH THEM SO GO OUT AND START CREATING. LIFE IS SHORT. LIVE YOUR DREAM, AND WEAR YOUR PASSION.

Holstee drew initial attention to itself with this "manifesto," which has been shared by millions through social media.

INCONSISTENCIES IN YOUR STORY

Inconsistencies in your story and about who you are as a company can be devastating to a brand; they can tarnish your reputation and cause people to feel uncertain about your legitimacy and integrity.

We've even seen this happen with great brands that we love, for example Shea Moisture. Shea has an incredible brand story that is printed right on the package for the whole world to see:

> *Sofi Tucker began selling shea nuts at the village market in Bonthe, Sierra Leone, in 1912. By age 19, the widowed mother of four was selling her shea butter and African black soap all over the countryside. Sofi Tucker was our grandmother, and Shea Moisture is her legacy. We proudly create culturally-authentic, time-tested skin and hair care remedies from family recipes using all-natural and fair trade ingredients.*

Shea Moisture has a fiercely loyal fan base of more than 66,700 on Facebook and more than 11,000 Twitter followers. The brand has dozens of consumer-generated videos on YouTube, with thousands of page views each, offering tips and extolling the brand's transformative effects. Shea Moisture is very active in social media and responsive to its loyal fans, who often share before-and-after pictures of their hair and stories of their skin revivals. In December 2012 the company even created a special holiday pop-up shop in New York City's Bryant Park to bring its story to life. Sounds good, right?

For more than **one year**, this has been the company's home page:

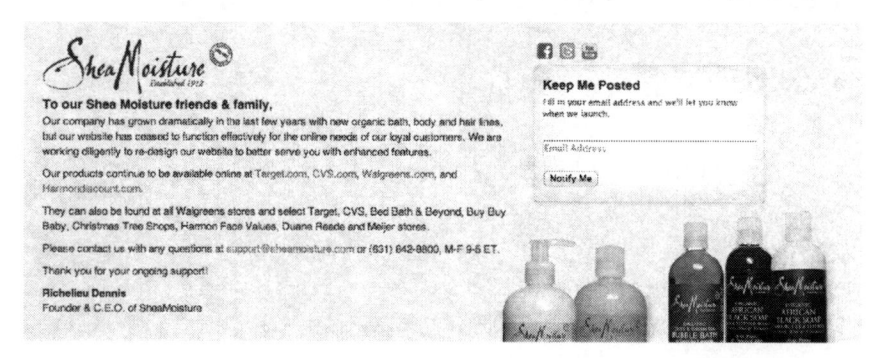

So while Shea Moisture is active in social media, creating retail outposts, and expanding its product line into stores such as Target and CVS, its website is basically a static placeholder. We get a splash page, apologizing for the lack of a website and citing that the company is "working diligently to redesign our website to better serve you with enhanced features."

Ironically the company also spends thousands (likely hundreds of thousands) of dollars on print ads in national fashion and beauty magazines, which — get this — direct people to the website ... which apologizes for the lack of a website! Why is this company spending all of this money on print advertising that sends people to a website that doesn't exist? This makes no sense.

Although the products can be purchased online at other retailers, there is no excuse for a successful, popular brand's website to be down for more than a year with the same note. This is a serious flaw in Shea Moisture's story line. If the company can't even fix its own website, it makes us – as consumers – wonder whether its products are really as wonderful and authentic as we think they are (and that Shea claims they are). Aren't you curious as to what's really going on behind the scenes when a website promises that a company is working "diligently" on an issue to better serve customers? It doesn't sound very convincing, or consistent, to us.

SHEER ADVICE: HOW TO MAINTAIN CONSISTENCY

CREATE A CONTENT STYLE GUIDE

Many brands have a style guide that includes design and visual guidelines to identify color palettes, logo iterations, and usage and imagery guidelines for a completely consistent brand identity. We recommend that every business also create a Content Style Guide (CSG) as an essential first step to delivering a consistent message.

A CSG not only sets the foundation for website content and all other content initiatives, it also captures the details about your company all in one place. A CSG should be continually updated as your company evolves, and reviewed annually to make sure it's still accurate. This helpful guide can be used internally to ensure that all marketing messages are on the right track and that your audience is clearly defined. It also can be given to any contract or new employee so they have a clear understanding of your company from the start. After all, your employees are your greatest brand storytellers.

A CSG helps you zero-in on the core ideas and strengths that distinguish your brand from the competition with words that carve out your unique position. It guides your storytelling by creating a resource that defines your tone, voice, and message. Your CSG can be as detailed as you'd like to capture all of the essential elements of who you are. Here are some suggestions of topics to include:

About

This section is simply a factual reference to the who, what, when, where, and why of your brand. Think about this section as your company overview. How would you describe your business to a new employee? What important facts do they need to know to understand why your brand exists?

Message Hierarchy

Your message hierarchy captures the essence of what you want to say and communicate. It identifies your key brand messages in order of importance and should set a standard to be used in all content. In this section, define and prioritize the most important messages and key points you are trying to communicate as a brand. Sticking to this order of hierarchy will set the standard for communication in design and content across all channels.

Voice & Tone

A strong voice can create movements ("I had a dream") and change history ("I do"). A clear voice identifies brands ("Just do it") and sells services ("What's in your wallet?"). Your voice is who you are. If your best friend used a different voice every time you talked, you might think he or she was losing it; however, companies often make the mistake of speaking from an inconsistent voice or perspective. How will you speak to your audience? Is your brand professional, funny, serious, clever? Is your brand's personality light and friendly, serious, informative? Will you post and respond from the first person ("I"), or from a personal, yet collective "we"?

Your voice and tone define choices in style, diction, and terminology. It should set a standard to be used in all content, even in design elements and when someone from your team responds to questions in social media. Include any grammar or language guidelines specific to your brand, as well as things to avoid (e.g., "never speak in the first person" or "never use negative examples").

Buyer Personas

A persona is not just another marketing buzzword, but a useful and strategic tool that will help you connect to people in a meaningful way. Buyer personas are representations of the real people that your products and services are for. They should represent both your current customers, as well as prospects that can turn into customers if you create the right content that speaks to them and shows that you understand their needs.

This section of the CSG will help you steer away from one-size-fits-all content, or worse, content that's all about you. It helps you focus on insights and behavior instead of just demographics.

There are many good resources out there that can teach you about the art and science of creating buyer personas. Marketing author and speaker David Meerman Scott advises that buyer personas can completely transform all of your marketing, and that creating a content strategy around your buyer personas is more effective than going on and on about your company. In his well-known book, *The New Rules of Marketing & PR*, he writes:

> "A buyer persona represents a distinct group of potential customers or an archetypal person whom you want your marketing to reach ... By

truly understanding the market problems that your products and services solve for your buyer personas, you transform your marketing from mere product specific, egocentric gobbledygook that only you understand and care about into valuable information that people are eager to consume and that they use to make the choice to do business with your organization."[8]

Another great resource on buyer personas is the Buyer Persona Institute (www.buyerpersona.com), developed by Adele Revella, which is dedicated to the art and science of creating buyer personas.

Beyond the typical "Madison Avenue" list that defines target audiences by factors such as household income, gender, and geography, here are just a few of the many insightful questions that your buyer personas could answer, depending on the nature of your products or services:

- What is their daily life like?
- What is their personality – are they shy, outgoing, etc.?
- How do they find information?
- What is their job function?
- What do you offer them to make their lives easier/better in some way?

Services/Products

This section should include a list of every product or service your company offers and to whom you offer them. This may sound easy for you to do — and hopefully it is — but it is essential to list these in one place and define each element.

A CSG will help you create an authentic voice that stays consistent across all communications and clearly speaks to your intended audience. It will also help you avoid speaking in industry jargon and catchphrases (we're the best, fastest, smartest!) that really say nothing about who you are.

CREATE AN EDITORIAL CALENDAR

With all of the opportunities that brands have to share their story comes the risk of sending out mixed messages. Most businesses aren't using just one channel or platform to tell their story; they're likely using up to a dozen or more, including Facebook, Twitter, Google+, Quora, Pinterest, LinkedIn, YouTube, email, white papers, e-newsletters, webinars, and a blog to name a few. In fact, according to the Content Marketing Institute, B2B North American marketers were using an average of 12 individual tactics in 2013.[9]

With all of the opportunities available, it can feel challenging to create continuity across all of these platforms. To avoid becoming disjointed in the telling of your story, you need a plan and a schedule for how you will execute across the different channels. Holding your business accountable to a scheduled editorial calendar helps your blog stay on track with relevant posts, keeps your Facebook page updated with engaging content, and makes your daily "to-do" list manageable.

Editorial calendars didn't just pop up overnight. They have been around for quite a while in print media such as newspapers and magazines. The traditional editorial calendar is simply a schedule that keeps track of stories and articles from concept to development to publishing. Editorial calendars keep printing schedules consistent, so publications can make deadlines and plan the best content for their readers.

An editorial calendar for your business has the same goal. Anyone who publishes information to any platform (print, online, video, etc.) can use an editorial calendar to keep topics organized and distribution on schedule. Editorial calendars that integrate a keyword strategy also help your products and services rank well in search engines. You can use an editorial calendar for newsletters, websites, blogs, and any other content that you publish regularly. It just takes a little strategic editorial planning to get you into the flow of things.

- What information does your audience want to learn about?
- What does your company offer that makes their lives easier/better?
- What channels are the best to communicate through?

Here are some editorial calendar tools to check out, many of which are free or have a free trial to help you begin your experiment:

- **Kapost** (http://kapost.com/) — Built specifically for content marketers, this platform lets you manage multiple contributors and includes an online payment system. It also incorporates a distribution and analysis system.

- **WordPress** (http://wordpress.org/extend/plugins/editorial-calendar/) — WordPress has a handy editorial calendar plugin that helps keep blog posts organized and on-schedule. This is a good solution if you are focusing on a blog, but it doesn't have many features for multiple users or incorporating other types of content. It is free and very easy to install.

- **Compendium** (http://www.compendium.com/) — Compendium takes the entire content marketing lifecycle into account, including the editorial aspects of a content calendar. It has a place to store topics, assign timelines, monitor tasks, and track results.

- **GatherContent** (http://www.gathercontent.com/) — GatherContent is more of an "in-the cloud" content collaboration tool that keeps all content in one place rather than relying on multiple versions of Word docs being passed back and forth. It's ideal for teams that want to collaborate on content before publishing it to the Web.

- **DivvyHQ** (http://www.divvyhq.com/) — DivvyHQ has a helpful feature called Parking Lot where you can store all of those great ideas that come flowing to you throughout the day. It also allows for multiple calendars that can connect to a master to give you a bird's-eye view of your content needs.

- **Excel** — Don't overlook the simplicity of an Excel spreadsheet when considering the best editorial calendar options for your team. If you're just getting started with content marketing and looking for an affordable, easy option, Excel can be an effective solution.

The main purpose of an editorial calendar is to ensure consistency in content delivery and messaging, while making sure your content has a plan and a purpose to help you achieve your goals.

CHOOSE THE RIGHT CHANNELS

Many marketers set up a blog, Facebook page, Twitter profile, and LinkedIn account. Then, they read an article about Pinterest and join Google+ on a whim and think their content marketing is taking off with a bang. Instead, all that bangs is their head against their desk as hours of each day are spent trying to create and manage conversations in five different communities. How do you choose where to share your story?

1. **Start by looking at how your target market** connects and communicates. Do they participate and ask questions on Facebook, LinkedIn, Google+? Do they research before making purchasing decisions and look for guidance on websites and blogs? Do they want to stay informed and subscribe to e-newsletters? Are they more comfortable with print pieces (e.g., brochures, sell sheets, postcards)? Go to where your audience lives.

2. **Examine your goals.** If you're trying to drive traffic to your site, consider ramping up your website content and starting a blog. If you want to increase conversions, consider lead-generating options such as free guides, e-books, or digital downloads.

3. **Consider your resources.** If you're getting pressure to participate in social media or start a blog, but don't have the time or financial resources to update with informative content on a regular basis, don't do it! Instead, focus more on setting a really good foundation with your website content or start a monthly newsletter. The point is to focus on the types of content that you can maintain on a consistent basis.

Remember, not every single company in the world should be on every channel. You do not have to use something just because it exists! In fact, only a handful of brands have a strong, consistent presence in every single touch point they enter (think Google, Coke, and Starbucks). You do not have to be on Facebook! Your brand might fall on deaf ears on Twitter. And no one may show up at your Hangout on Google+. Doing more than you can handle or being in the wrong place for your brand will put a huge crack in your foundation and place a serious strain on your efforts to be authentic.

CLEAR CONCLUSION

Consistent brands are seen as the most trusted. To achieve this trust level, you have to tell the same, authentic story in each channel you participate in. The most effective brands maintain a brand style, plan out their content, and strategically choose the best content platforms to reach their target markets.

CHAPTER 4
Create Customer and Employee Evangelists: Trust Others To Do the Talking

"Do what you do so well, that people can't resist telling others about you."
—Walt Disney

The desire for humans to share information is not new. People have been sharing information since the days of messenger pigeons and telegraphs. The case could probably be made that cave drawings set the foundation for today's infographics.

In the business world we share files, contacts, and leads. In yoga class we share space. At the dinner table we share stories. Radio, television, the Internet … they were all created for sharing information. Parents ask kids to share. Teachers ask students to share. Marketers ask prospects and clients to share. It's no wonder that social media channels are continually part of our daily lives.

When people are passionate about the businesses they interact with in their life, they want to tell others. Often, companies feel they need to be the drivers of conversation about their business and fear letting their customers speak for them, when actually, people who love a company's products and services are the greatest, most authentic marketers.

In their groundbreaking book *Creating Customer Evangelists*, Jackie Huba and Ben McConnell clearly explain why evangelists are your best sales team: "They know your target audience better than you because they are the target audience!"[1]

WHY BRAND EVANGELISTS?

According to a 2010 Satmetrix study, evangelists spend 13 percent more than the average customer and refer business equal to 45 percent of the money they spend![2] HubSpot says that consumers are 71 percent more likely to buy a product after a connection's recommendation on a social media channel.[3] In a time when there are more than 180 million blogs in the world, 1 billion people on Facebook, and 500 million people on Twitter, the opportunity for companies to develop brand evangelists has never been greater.

Brand evangelists — or advocates — are loyalists who are so passionate about certain brands that they'll market to others without any personal gain. They form emotional attachments to brands, becoming cheerleaders who recommend products and services to family, friends, and anyone else who will listen. Brand evangelists tell a personal story, which is often more impactful than a brand telling its own story.

> *"People don't believe what you tell them.*
> *They rarely believe what you show them.*
> *They often believe what their friends tell them.*
> *They always believe what they tell themselves."*
> —Seth Godin, Entrepreneur, Author, and Public Speaker

Finding and developing relationships with loyal customers gives businesses of all sizes a direct connection to their fan base. These followers can be more authentic advocates for telling the brand's story than the company could ever be.

HOW THEY DO IT...
BRAND EVANGELISTS

How do companies convince customers to not only use their products, but also to advocate for a product and "own" it as part of their identities? How do you get people so excited that they're willing to put a sticker on their car — or even a tattoo on their body — of a brand, as Harley-Davidson owners often do? More importantly, how do you find those people who might be your brand's best-kept secret?

Being transparent, delivering on promise, and making emotional connections are the qualities that enable you to transform customers into brand evangelists. Companies that create these powerful relationships with people are adept at delivering a consistent message and brand story, and making themselves indispensable in people's lives.

> *Richard Sears was a storytelling revolutionary and an originator of many marketing firsts. One of Sears' most genius achievements was turning his customers into brand evangelists. He sent a letter to the best Sears customers in Iowa and asked them to give out 24 catalogs. If their friends became customers, he rewarded these "volunteer salespeople" with a stove, bicycle, or a sewing machine! To encourage repeat customers, Sears initiated one of the first customer loyalty programs, now a staple of many brands, where customers were given a one-dollar certificate for every dollar spent with the retailer. Consumers could then redeem these certificates for specific items.*

Brands that have earned copious brand evangelists are those that are trusted and valued, and create a sense of community and belonging. These traits set the foundation for leveraging advocacy, which brands can support through different tools and customer programs.

You can't fake brand evangelism. But, to get customers to advocate for your brand, you have to live up to promises and exceed their expectations.

Maker's Mark

Maker's Mark has an "embassy" on its website where brand loyalists can register to become "ambassadors." The brand makes it fun and easy to have honorable status with the company and makes you feel like you're part of something special.

Bill Samuels, Jr., chairman emeritus of Maker's Mark, explains the philosophy behind the whiskey company's ambassador program: "We enjoy talking to our customers one-to-one. It really is in our nature. We never worry about the fact that this is inefficient, because we are only talking to 50 or 60 or a thousand or ten thousand instead of a million — which you do when you try to slap everybody on the ass with an advertising message. Because we know that our next customers are going to come from their efforts, not from our efforts."[4]

Does Maker's Mark actually listen to its ambassadors? Decide for yourself: In 2013, the company announced that in order to keep up with product demand, it was going to reduce the alcohol content in its whiskey. Word got out and prompted an onslaught of bitter (okay … angry) Tweets and Facebook posts. Maker's Mark fans decided they would rather have a shortage than an altered product. Three days later, Maker's Mark thanked its followers and promised to keep the recipe intact.

Bill Samuels, Jr., and his son Rob Samuels, the company's current COO, issued a statement that said: "We're humbled by your overwhelming response and passion for Maker's Mark. While we thought we were doing what's right, this is your brand and you told us in large numbers to change our decision."

Brand evangelists will not only speak for your brand, but speak up when you screw up.

Weed Pro Lawn Care

Ohio-based Weed Pro Lawn Care decided to reward its most loyal customers after recognizing that they were the ones who most often recommended the company to friends and family. Why not make these happy customers even happier?

Weed Pro's approach was to use a Net Promoter Score (NPS) to help gauge the likelihood that a customer would refer the company. It identified customers who gave the company a score of 9 or 10 as key brand evangelists, and created a customer engagement program to communicate with them via HubSpot. This important customer base received a specific email campaign encouraging them to refer their friends and family to Weed Pro, and each name received a follow-up call thanking them for their business.

In an article in *Direct Marketing News*, Weed Pro's Shaun Kanary said, "We put great customers up on a pedestal to help us generate leads."[5] In approximately six months, Weed Pro secured 49 new customers, 10 of whom came from this loyalty referral program — numbers far exceeding where they would normally be during that time of year.

Aleysai Beverage Corporation

In 2005, Aleysai Beverage Corporation (ABC), a Saudi Arabian soft drink company, began to explore the idea of developing an energy drink. At that time, local and imported energy drinks flooded the Saudi market, but Red Bull dominated as the inventor of the category. Red Bull had more publicity globally and, to the Saudi market, was the brand that serviced the higher clout of society even though the price point was the same as most imported brands. The leader in the local category of energy drinks was Bison, which had no point of differentiation from the look and feel of Red Bull, but was sold at a 60 percent lower price.

ABC decided to take an opposite approach than other energy drinks in the category. The first thing it did was to not name the product anything animal-related. The name they chose was Code Red. The brand moved away from the traditional blue and silver colors of the energy drink category, which Red Bull had introduced and every other brand followed. Code Red was packaged in vibrant red to make an impact on the shelf and stand out. ABC also chose to target the middle- and lower-tiers of the marketplace and distribute in less mainstream areas that most energy drinks neglected.

That was the start of the brand's relationship with the public. Besides being a Saudi-created drink, different in look and tone from other energy drinks, Code Red became a local hero, an underdog brand that fulfilled an unmet need through great taste and a lower price. This created an emotional connection with the Saudi people; it was a drink by them and for them. Even when competitors raised prices and introduced more SKUs, Code Red remained the same: one single proposition with the same look and taste.

Code Red didn't spend any money on marketing or advertising; its fan base spread the word for free. The brand maintained a humble positioning, and didn't even invest in a website. Because the core audience felt that the brand belonged to them, the consumers initiated several fan-based platforms to promote and support the product.

The brand grew from an authentic fan base of advocates. In fact, Code Red has an active Facebook page — with more than 5,000 fans — that was started and is managed entirely by a fan. There is a very small mention in one of the first posts that the page is entirely "fan maintained" and the brand does not interfere to try to control it in any way:

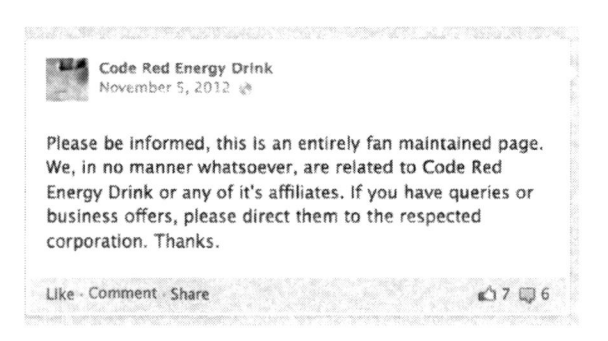

> **Code Red Energy Drink**
> November 5, 2012
>
> Please be informed, this is an entirely fan maintained page. We, in no manner whatsoever, are related to Code Red Energy Drink or any of it's affiliates. If you have queries or business offers, please direct them to the respected corporation. Thanks.
>
> Like · Comment · Share   👍 7 💬 6

But the passion is obvious:

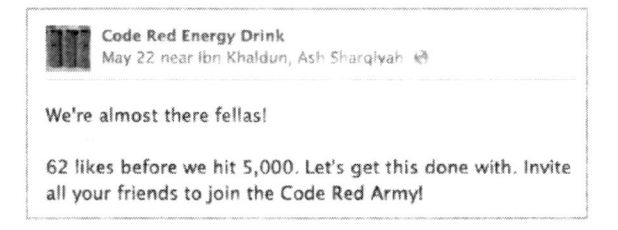

> **Code Red Energy Drink**
> May 22 near Ibn Khaldun, Ash Sharqiyah
>
> We're almost there fellas!
>
> 62 likes before we hit 5,000. Let's get this done with. Invite all your friends to join the Code Red Army!

Code Red simply remained a brand that was strong, yet silent, and the people gave it a voice. The customers who love Code Red became its ambassadors, endorsing it and recommending it to friends. Code Red is known as the "People's Drink."

(On a side note, because there was no marketing investment, Code Red's wholesalers and retailers benefited from higher margins and profitability, and Code Red has become a force to reckon with in the Middle Eastern energy drink category.)

The Chopping Block

The Chopping Block, a recreational cooking school and gourmet retail store in Chicago, built its community around enthusiastic home cooks and like-minded local foodies. Most relationships start with a cooking class. Some students attend a class and write a post about it on their personal blog, which the company usually learns about from a Google alert or Twitter.

The Chopping Block always gives back the love and reposts the link on all of its social media channels. This is great exposure for the blogger to a foodie community, plus The Chopping Block gets to share a positive story from one of its customers. Since The Chopping Block is all about getting people to cook at home, it tries to engage people in conversations about cooking in order to determine the obstacles they face.

One of its students, Tim Nickerson, regularly blogs about cooking classes he's taken and recipes he tries at home. Here's one of his posts:

Source: http://landtt.blogspot.com/2012/02/midnight-in-paris-class-at-chopping.html

The Chopping Block regularly interacts through Google+. One day Tim posed a question, asking about the difference between a chutney and a relish. Public Relations Director Andrea Miller saw the question and consulted with the company's chefs to answer him. Tim then posted about the answer:

"This response cracks me up – not because of the content, but the delivery. The first line: "Our experts have convened" – I envision this two ways. The first, at a regular staff meeting this question is posed to the chefs and a heated debate follows. The second option, someone goes to Google and finds the best/first answer and responds.

"These people are great, whether they took time to either discuss and create a really perfect response – or they took time to go to Google and piecemeal this together. No offense guys…

"Either way, I'm happy. Their answer makes perfect sense and it really does fit with what I thought and other friends have suggested."

Source: http://landtt.blogspot.com/2012/10/a-chutney-or-relish.html

According to Shelley Young, owner of The Chopping Block, Tim is now a brand ambassador for the company. "The relationship was truly derived from simply having a conversation about cooking, listening, and providing valuable content and excellent customer service. We also believe that food is a catalyst for friendship … we promote that philosophy with intimate classes and a low key atmosphere."

Lego

A smart, informed customer service rep is one of the most valuable employees a company can have. In 2013, a seven-year-old boy, Luka Apps, saved up his Christmas money to buy the Lego Ninjago Ultra Sonic Raider set. Not following his dad's advice, Luka took his new

Chapter 4: Create Customer and Employee Evangelists: Trust Others To Do the Talking

Lego companion, minifigure Jay ZX, with him when they went out to run errands. What do you think happened? Jay ZX went missing. Luka's wise dad suggested that he write to Lego for help. So, he sent an email to the company (likely with his dad's help) asking for a replacement. This is what the letter said:[6]

> Hello,
>
> My name is Luka Apps and I am seven years old.
>
> With all my money I got for Christmas I bought the Ninjago kit of the Ultrasonic Raider. The number is 9449. It is really good.
>
> My Daddy just took me to Sainsburys and told me to leave the people at home but I took them and I lost Jay ZX at the shop as it fell out of my coat.
>
> I am really upset I have lost him. Daddy said to send you a [sic] email to see if you will send me another one.
>
> I promise I won't take him to the shop again if you can.
>
> Luka

Luka received a reply from a Lego customer service rep named Richard. He told Luka that he spoke to Sensei Wu, a master from the Ninjago line, about the situation. Here is an excerpt from his response:

> Luka,
>
> ...Sensei Wu also told me it was okay if I sent you a new Jay and told me it would be okay if I included something extra for you because anyone that saves their Christmas money to buy the Ultrasonic Raider must be a really big Ninjago fan.
>
> So, I hope you enjoy your Jay minifigure with all his weapons. You will actually have the only Jay minifigure that combines 3 different Jays into one! I am also going to send you a bad guy for him to fight! Just remember, what Sensei Wu said: keep your minifigures protected like the Weapons of Spinjitzu! And, of course, always listen to your Dad.

Richard's email went viral throughout social media channels and generated amazing positive PR for Lego. As a result, the building block company earned even more brand evangelists … with Luka and his dad most certainly at the top of the list.

WHY EMPLOYEE EVANGELISTS?

> *"The indispensable employee brings humanity and connection and art to her organization. She is the key player, the one who's difficult to live without, the person you can build something around."*[7]
> —*Seth Godin,* **Linchpin**

You can have all of the external brand evangelists in the world, but if your own employees won't sing your praises, you have bigger problems to worry about.

Employee evangelists are some of the greatest cheerleaders a company can have. They are the ones who come face-to-face with customers and vendors and often serve as your front line of communication. From the receptionist to the CEO to your Twitter feed, everyone has the opportunity to make an impression and share your story. A brand's employees are some of its primary storytellers and ambassadors.

So much of the love that people have for brands comes from the people who represent it, so brand evangelism must ooze from the inside out. In the book *Brains on Fire*, authors Robbin Phillips, Greg Cordell, Geno Church, and Spike Jones talk enthusiastically about the need for passion inside an organization in order to create passion outside of it:

> *"If there's passion inside the company — from the very top to the good folks on the front lines — then you're easily going to find passion outside your company. But if your people are coming to work just to collect a paycheck, then you're not finding much passion inside or outside your walls."*

The authors propose an interesting question: *"If we randomly chose one of your employees and one of your customers and put them in a room together, would a passionate brand lovefest break out between these two strangers?"*[8]

Think about it. Would your employee and customer share the same feelings about your brand and tell the same story? Would they be kindred spirits, part of the same community? Pairing these two people would give you a true glimpse into not only how transparent your brand is in telling your story, but also how consistently you are telling it inside and outside the company walls.

Every employee in your business is a representation of you and your brand. They can build and grow — or damage — your brand story with each customer interaction. Each one of them must live out your brand promise and truly understand what makes your company tick.

HOW THEY DO IT...
EMPLOYEE EVANGELISTS
Zingerman's

Zingerman's, a family of food, café, and gourmet businesses in the Ann Arbor, Michigan area, grew from a small deli into a $45 million tour de force by teaching its employees to understand a P&L statement. Founded in 1982 as a small corner deli, Zingerman's transformed from a mom-and-pop shop into a business venture comprised of eight unique establishments with more than 500 employees.

Zingerman's recipe for success was a simple formula of impeccable customer service, open book management, and employee ownership policies. The real zinger? It teaches its employees about business, which increases their buy-in to the brand.

Zingerman's believes in the passion and spirit of its businesses more than the bottom line. The company's co-founder and CEO Ari Weinzweig has said:

"It makes no sense to have wide receivers and not teach them how football works. I would argue that 99 percent of the workforce are making decisions that we feel are stupid (at an executive level) because we never taught them how business works."

Dubbed "the coolest small company in America" by *Inc.*,[9] and "one of the top 25 world's best food markets" by *Food & Wine*,[10] Zingerman's also has been lauded in the *Harvard Business Review* and on MSNBC for its business practices and customer and employee programs. In fact, it has launched another business venture, ZingTrain, which educates and trains other businesses on creating cultures based on customer service and employee value. ZingTrain seminars represent the company's philosophy: "Fun, Flavorful Finance: Why Our Dishwashers Know Our Net Operating Profit."

FreshBooks

FreshBooks, an online invoicing and time-tracking software company serving contractors, businesses, and agencies, is known for its employee and brand evangelists. An article in the *Financial Post* cited FreshBooks employee Melina Stathopoulos as one of the company's top employee evangelists. She said:

"Everybody here talks about FreshBooks all the time ... we're out there advocating for our brand, talking about it with friends and with family members, and getting the word out there."[11]

The great sense of employee pride at FreshBooks is commonly attributed to co-founder and CEO Mike McDerment. He is the head cheerleader of the company culture, one that offers on-site ping pong tables, parties, video games, social clubs, and an annual offsite retreat.

One of the unifying factors at FreshBooks is that all staff members, no matter their level or role, spend the first month of employment doing customer service, manning the phones and offering support, in order to personally understand the foundation and nature of the company.

FreshBooks not only has an internal force of brand ambassadors, but is also known for being one of the first companies to use Twitter as a customer service tool, creating a legion of customer brand evangelists in the process. One of the most famous stories of FreshBooks' groundbreaking customer service via social media happened (way back) in 2008. One of its users, @chelpixie, a Boston-based virtual assistant, had apparently been stood up by her date and tweeted out her disappointment. Well, FreshBooks was listening and responded with this:

> @chelpixie - we would never stand you up
> 08:54 AM May 29, 2008 from web in reply to chelpixie
>
> **freshbooks**
> Freshbooks

This very nice acknowledgment was not enough for the FreshBooks social media team. Not only did they send her a shout out, and likely a smile, the next day they sent her flowers! Imagine receiving flowers from a company you do business with over a comment made on Twitter?

This honest gesture by FreshBooks set the precedent for its ongoing tone of authenticity, which still carries on today. Its team certainly created at least one brand evangelist for life, and likely many others as a result of its friendly, human response.

WHEN THE TABLES TURN

Sometimes, a company will do something to make even its most loyal evangelists turn on them. Products not living up to expectations? Change in materials? Services not on par? PR snafu handled poorly? Dishonest responses? Changing company policies? Ignoring comments on social media? All of these things play a role in holding up a brand's integrity and keeping its internal and external evangelist army marching strong and proud.

Hewlett-Packard

We know someone, let's call her Kelly. Now, Kelly was an avid HP evangelist for years. We heard about HP this … and HP that … and how there was no other. Kelly was a huge HP advocate, until … she got stuck with a defective laptop. Kelly received a laptop made of poor quality plastic parts that certainly didn't live up to her high expectations and experiences with HP products until that point. Six months later, when the cheap frame around the screen fell apart, customer service insinuated that she broke it! Well, that took care of that. "So I became a Dell person," Kelly says. "But now, even after having gone through several great Dells, I'm even gun-shy to talk *them* up!"

Be honest with your very important brand evangelists so they don't transfer their loyalties to someone else, and likely tell everyone about the error of your ways in the process. If you don't turn your back on your customers, they won't turn on you. If HP had been honest, owning up to its mistake in downgrading parts to less expensive plastic, the company would still have a strong brand evangelist on its team, and likely many others.

SHEER ADVICE: HOW TO CREATE BRAND EVANGELISTS

Showing interest in the people who are talking about you is essential to converting customers into brand evangelists and storytellers. In order to get customers to advocate your brand, you have to exceed their expectations. Once you identify these people, give them something special (and we don't mean cash … get creative). If it's special enough, they'll likely tell the world.

Define your brand evangelists. Before you can engage with them, you have to decide what makes a brand evangelist. Is it the number of retweets, comments on posts, shares, likes, or pins? Is it a customer's purchasing history? Is it all of your newsletter subscribers? There are lots of different factors that can make someone a brand evangelist, so decide what the right mix is for your brand.

Engage with influencers. Whether industry experts, authors, bloggers, or highly followed thought leaders in social media, "influencers" are people who can provide another voice for your product or service. These people can write a blog post or article about you; promote or share information about you through social media channels; or allow you to guest post on their widely read and respected blog or online publication.

Listen and respond! To find people who are advocating for your brand and telling your story, LISTEN. Social media has given businesses more voices – those of the evangelists who sing the praises of their products and services and recommend them to friends and family. Pay attention to the people who are on your Facebook page. Find out who follows your brand on Twitter, Pinterest, LinkedIn, and Google+, and who subscribes to your YouTube channel.

Identify people who are already choosing to hear what you have to say as a starting point. Monitor conversations to identify who is praising your brand, where, and to whom. You may find people who are influencers in an industry, or others who are peer influencers among a group of friends or in their community.

And, for goodness' sake, respond! There is nothing worse than when a person or company ignores people who ask questions or leave comments that deserve a response. Whether positive or negative, every question should be addressed, even if it's just to direct someone to a specific email address or phone number for more information.

If you don't reply to people, what does that say about your authenticity as a brand? Every time someone contacts you via social media, think of it as your phone ringing. Would you ignore your customer service line all day … or even for weeks at a time? When you do respond, lose the canned responses. Be genuine, acknowledge the issues, and show that you care.

> **Brands on Facebook are Falling Short**
> According to a 2012 A.T. Kearney Social Media Study,[12] 48 of the top 50 brands have a Facebook presence, but are not using it to boost brand engagement. The study showed that 38 out of the 50 brands only allowed posts from the company on their Facebook pages. Huh? Isn't the goal of Facebook to engage in two-way conversation with your biggest fans? The study also showed that when consumers contacted brands via social media, 27 out of the 50 never responded and only four out of 50 responded to more than a quarter of the comments or questions they received. Mind-boggling.

Identify your partners. Brands evangelizing other brands is very powerful. Do you partner with other companies on projects or share a similar philosophy with another company you're friendly with? Showing your support of another business — especially small, midsize, and local — will often get the favor returned.

Get involved. Participate in the conversation about your industry or brand. Join conversations where you can add value in channels such as Twitter, LinkedIn, Google+, and industry blogs. Answer questions and talk to the people who are interested in your brand and your industry.

Treat your evangelists like the media. While *The New York Times* may reach a bigger audience, industry blogs and fan sites will give you direct access to your advocates. Offer them breaking information, the opportunity to submit a product review, or an invitation to visit your offices.

Thank them. Let's say, you "overhear" Jill from L.A. raving about your vineyard's wine on Facebook. You'd look like a stalker if you jumped in and made a comment on the spot, and the conversation would end there. But what if you were to contact her directly and offer her a bottle of wine, an invitation to a local tasting, or a tour of your vineyard? Or what if you just said THANK YOU, let her know how much you appreciate her support, and gave her the scoop on some new varieties? Most evangelists don't want to be compensated, but often a thank you or a deeper insight into your brand (a tour, new samples, etc.) will go a long way.

SHEER ADVICE:
HOW TO CREATE EMPLOYEE EVANGELISTS

As we've said, evangelism should burst at the seams of your organization and flow from the inside out. A lot of the love that people have for brands comes from those who are behind the scenes and on the front lines. Imagine if your employees were naturally advocating for your brand in their social media channels, at parties, and in dinner conversations.

Accentuate the positive. Instill positivity, open communication, transparency, and a staff-oriented culture. Supportive environments lead to greater customer service and employee retention. Employee evangelists take pride in what they are helping to create because they live it every day.

Be a great role model. It all trickles down from the top. It's not surprising that many of the most evangelized brands (e.g., Apple, Starbucks, and Zappos) have highly visible, public, and charismatic leaders who set the tone for the company culture and act as leaders of the evangelist army.

Get out of their way. Many companies, especially enterprise-level organizations, have rules, guidelines, and layers of red tape that hold employees back from evangelizing. While policies and procedures are necessary for social media (for regulatory and legal reasons), do it within reason. Facilitate, but don't restrain to the point of oppressiveness. That's a big part of maintaining a transparent organization — have control, but also have restraint.

Create a community. Give your internal influencers a voice. Foster a community of open communication, connect people on different teams, promote the sharing of ideas, and tear down department lines. Everyone should be able to easily connect — energizing and supporting across job functions and levels.

CLEAR CONCLUSION

Letting brand evangelists speak for your products and services is one of the most authentic ways you can market your company. You can't force people to become brand evangelists inside or outside of your organization. Brand evangelists are created organically when employees take pride in being a part of something they believe in.

The best way to create brand evangelists is to truly engage with your audience. When you develop an honest relationship by communicating, showing your human side, and expressing appreciation, brand evangelists will proudly tell your story for you.

CHAPTER 5
Listen, Respond & Deal with Negativity: Have Honest Conversations with Customers and Yourself

"Your brand is what other people say about you when you're not in the room."
—*Jeff Bezos, Founder, Amazon*

Today, we prefer authenticity to perfection from the brands that we choose to do business with. Fans, friends, and even foes want to see and hear from the real you. They don't want canned corporate responses, publicist sound bites, obviously fake excuses, or worse, the brush off.

If you're a performing artist, fans want to know if you're really sick or not quite up to taking the stage. If you're a brand in a social media crisis over a snafu on Twitter, consumers want you to address it honestly and professionally. If your audience knows where you're coming from, they will likely feel more connected to you and be more forgiving.

One of the most damaging things a brand can do is ignore its audience online when negative comments pop up or a crisis arises. It's inevitable that bad comes with the good, and facing the bad head on and remaining transparent is the only way to uphold your positive reputation. When you don't respond, it tarnishes your reputation in a similar way as the public relations "no-no" of responding to an answer with "no comment."

EVERYONE'S A CRITIC

"Hyper connectivity allows companies to be in that room now, 24/7. They can listen and even join the conversation."
—*Tim Leberecht, Chief Marketing Officer, NBBJ*

Negative comments and unhappy customers are unavoidable in the online space, where people can connect directly to brands and share their opinions without filters. Social media also creates opportunities for people to hide behind fake profiles and possibly make comments they wouldn't make if they weren't posting incognito.

Negative reviews and comments happen to the best of companies, even family-friendly Cheerios. Cheerios had to make a choice on how to deal with social media critics after they released a sweet commercial called "Just Checking" about a little girl trying to keep her dad's heart healthy. The little girl is bi-racial and what was intended as a family ad turned into a PR frenzy. After a bombardment of racial slurs, Cheerios disabled the video's comment section on YouTube a day after the ad appeared online.

Camille Gibson, the brand's vice president of marketing, said in a statement: "At Cheerios, we know there are many kinds of families, and we celebrate them all." Later, on *The TODAY Show*, she added: "The YouTube comments that were made were, in our view, not family-friendly. And that was really the trigger for us to pull them off."

Was it right for Cheerios to pull down the comments? Perhaps, but where does the censoring end? They also had to disable comments on a video called "Big Brother," presumably because the racists who could no longer comment on "Just Checking" moved their rant.

At least Cheerios responded and took some action. According to the 2012 A.T. Kearney Social Media Study, 27 out of 50 large brands never responded to comments at all.[1]

If your company doesn't have a team of qualified, trained people (or even one person) monitoring social media, you may likely find yourself in a position of damage control or — even worse — surprise, by not even knowing bad conversations are happening until there is a crisis on your hands. Pay attention! Remember, if you choose not to be involved in the conversation, it will happen without you. And no one likes to be talked about behind their back.

Chapter 5: Listen, Respond & Deal with Negativity: Have Honest Conversations with Customers and Yourself

WHAT IF?

It always irks us when hotels on TripAdvisor don't respond to negative comments. Honestly, it makes us feel that if they are ignoring the comment, then what the guest is saying must be true! Ignoring an ugly comment will not make it go away. And in the travel and tourism industry — one that is increasingly being impacted by customer reviews — hoteliers must respond to the less than stellar comments or concede to admitting they're true.

A phony bologna response doesn't help either. You know a manager will not be taking any action if the response sounds saccharine and canned like, "Thanks for your feedback. We are always working to improve our facilities."

What if, after seeing a negative review, a hotel not only responded authentically, but personally? For example, say a family stays at a hotel and the heated pool is broken. The mom writes a review about the hotel and the pool issues. What if the hotel manager went beyond a polite response like, "We are aware that our indoor pool was freezing last week and the problem has now been resolved," which really doesn't do much for the mom whose kids had blue lips and cried all afternoon because they couldn't swim in the awesome indoor pool.

What if the hotel responded to the negative review by letting the family know when the pool was fixed, offering a free night's stay, and asking them to try the hotel again? Imagine the positive review that might come from that mom after a "re-do" that ended great. Not to mention all of the people on TripAdvisor who would see the hotel's response and feel the real person behind the words. That's what earns a 4 or 5-star review instead of a 2 or 3.

HOW THEY DO IT

"I think brands are really naïve to think that they are in full control of their perception out there today. I think that with social media and the speed at which things travel today, there's no way to hide it."[2]
—*Jill Dumain, Director of Environmental Policy, Patagonia*

KitchenAid

KitchenAid faced a major social media crisis in October 2012, when an employee posted an inappropriate tweet (using the company's handle) about Barack Obama's grandmother during a Presidential debate. The tweet went out to 24,000 followers before it was quickly deleted.

KitchenAid immediately issued this apology:

> **KitchenAid**
> @KitchenAidUSA
>
> Deepest apologies for an irresponsible tweet that is in no way a representation of the brand's opinion. #nbcpolitics
>
> 3 Oct 12

The company's senior director of the KitchenAid brand, Cynthia Soledad, took to Twitter right away to respond to journalists, followers, and the President's family, stating sincere apologies and offering to talk on record about what happened. She also posted a message on the company's Facebook page and sent an email to Mashable that read:

> *"During the debate tonight, a member of our Twitter team mistakenly posted an offensive tweet from the KitchenAid handle instead of a personal handle. The tasteless joke in no way represents our values at KitchenAid, and that person won't be tweeting for us anymore. That said, I lead the KitchenAid brand, and I take responsibility for the whole team. I am deeply sorry to President Obama, his family, and the Twitter community for this careless error. Thanks for hearing me out."*[3]

While the damage was done, Cynthia was calm, quick, and professional. She didn't make it worse by ignoring the comment or pretending it didn't happen. There have been many brands, politicians, and celebrities that have claimed their accounts have been hacked, but Cynthia took personal responsibility immediately as the leader of the KitchenAid team and faced the issue completely transparently.

Domino's Pizza

On the flipside, Domino's Pizza in 2009 used negative comments to transform its brand. Domino's was quickly losing market share in the highly competitive pizza delivery market and conducted focus groups to hear what consumers really thought. The results were pretty dismal, including feedback such as the pizza was "rubber," "cardboard," and "made without love."

Domino's used the comments as fuel to its fire to reinvigorate the food and the brand. It used the feedback as a springboard to "do better" and "create pizza people will love." The team tried more than a dozen combinations of sauce, cheese, spices, and crusts to basically create a new recipe and reinvent the 50-year-old brand.

Domino's taped videos of the consumer focus groups and created a documentary showing real Domino's employees showing up at the homes of some of their consumer critics with the new and improved pizza. The company bravely created an entire website dedicated to the project with the header, "Did we actually face our critics and reinvent our pizza from the crust up? OH YES WE DID."

WHAT NOT TO DO

Negative reviews and comments can happen even to the best of companies. It's how you handle them — authentically and professionally — that can actually put you back on top. Learn by these examples of what not to do when a crisis arises.

Subway

Subway made headlines and was actually sued for failing to deliver an authentic experience. Like many other viral phenomena, the Subway scandal started with a Facebook post. Australian teen Matt Corby posted a photo of the "12-inch sub" he bought in Perth, Australia, which measured only 11 inches. He posted the picture on Subway Australia's Facebook page with the simple caption, "Subway pls respond," and the post rapidly received more than 100,000 Likes. The next day, Subway Australia responded with the allegation that

"Footlong" is merely a creative liberty and doesn't designate measurement.

After Matt's photo went viral, Subway customers worldwide started posting photos of their own inch-short subs. Four out of seven "Footlongs" purchased by the *New York Post* only measured 11 or 11.5 inches.

> With regards to the size of the bread and calling it a footlong, 'SUBWAY FOOTLONG' is a registered trademark as a descriptive name for the sub sold in Subway® Restaurants and not intended to be a measurement of length. The length of the bread baked in the restaurant cannot be assured each time as the proofing process may vary slightly each time in the restaurant.

This post has since been deleted by the company.

These complaints have led to lawsuits by customers in New Jersey, Pennsylvania, and Chicago. The Chicago plaintiff claims that his sandwich was less than 11 inches long and alleges a "pattern of fraudulent, deceptive, and otherwise improper advertising, sales, and marketing practices." Two New Jersey men filed a suit the same day seeking damages of more than $5 million. Both cases are seeking class-action status and will likely be combined if they move to the federal level.

Subway issued a statement saying that sandwiches will be more consistently 12 inches long:

> "We have redoubled our efforts to ensure consistency and correct length in every sandwich we serve ... Our commitment remains steadfast to ensure that every Subway Footlong sandwich is 12 inches at each location worldwide."[4]

Thanks to technology, even teenagers have the power to draw worldwide attention to false content and bring inauthenticity to light, when only national media outlets could before. People should be able to demand and expect the truth. And now, brands have to deliver on their promises and know that people won't settle for less than a real experience.

Lululemon

Lululemon, the Canadian lifestyle brand known for its workout clothes and running gear, pulled 17 percent of its stock off the shelves in one weekend after "realizing" the material was sheer to the point of being see-through, which is not the kind of transparency consumers crave. It announced the decision to customers in a blog post titled, "A Letter to Our Guests."[5] It also added a FAQ page to the Press Room on its site. At first glance, it may have seemed as if lululemon was reaching out and being transparent. The blog post begins with, "At lululemon, our most important relationship is with our communities and our guests. We recently learned some information about some product that arrived in our stores and we wanted you to know right away."

Dig a bit deeper, however, and the communication faded. The brand's Twitter feed spoke only to good times and happy days. Its Facebook page had plenty of posts from fans about the issue, but not a mention from the brand. One fan even called out lululemon with an article from *The Wall Street Journal* that quoted the brand's Taiwanese supplier as saying all shipments went through an approved certification process according to contract requirements. The response from lululemon? Crickets.

Since posting the "Letter to Our Guests," which is a rather impersonal title for such a beloved brand, nearly 85 people (so far) had left comments. Here are a few:

- Blog Comment: "I write this out of love for lulu. I used to be a huge, HUGE lulu fan. **But people have been writing about this for a while now** and it's disappointing to read that they 'recently' learned about it."

- Blog Comment: "It's great that you made a statement about the sheerness that some buyers can experience with some of your pants. But I think you made a mistake in saying that the only pants affected were a select group of black nylon ones. **I guess you have not been reading the comments on your product pages**, but EVERY pair of pants has at least a few comments on the declining quality of material."

The brand did respond about five times to the various comments, in a very corporate, bland tone. Come on lululemon, we all know you're going through a tough time. Use your words to remind us that you're human. Sure, you offered refunds or exchanges to customers who bought the affected product. Nice gesture, but how about letting your real fans know, and posting this information where they are trying to connect with you in social media?

Amy's Baking Company

We saved the best for last.

In 2013, this Scottsdale, Arizona, restaurant and bakery literally blew up across media channels through its own meltdown in social media. The company quickly gained notoriety not for its delicious baked goods and sandwiches, but because of the owners' highly eccentric and off-the-wall (okay, a little crazy) responses online to customer comments and criticisms.

In an episode of FOX's *Kitchen Nightmares* (there's a red flag for you), notoriously harsh Chef Gordon Ramsay, who normally unabashedly berates restaurant owners, could not convince Amy's Baking Company owners to change their ways. Ramsay actually walked out on them in the episode for being too difficult to work with. Their Yelp reviews should have been an easy indicator:

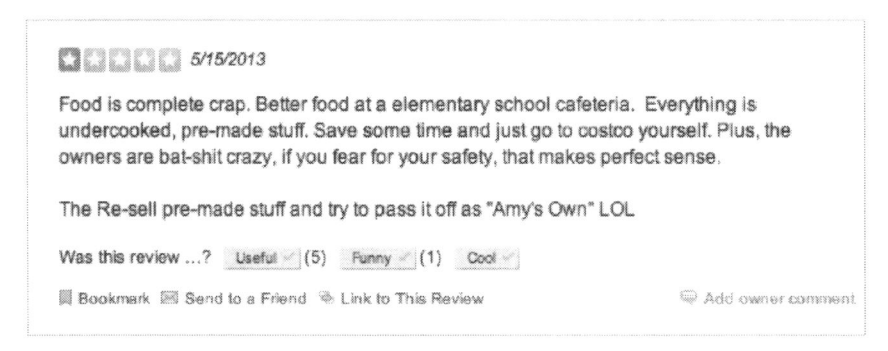

> ★☆☆☆☆ 5/15/2013
>
> Food is complete crap. Better food at a elementary school cafeteria. Everything is undercooked, pre-made stuff. Save some time and just go to costco yourself. Plus, the owners are bat-shit crazy, if you fear for your safety, that makes perfect sense.
>
> The Re-sell pre-made stuff and try to pass it off as "Amy's Own" LOL
>
> Was this review ...? Useful (5) Funny (1) Cool
>
> Bookmark Send to a Friend Link to This Review   Add owner comment

Redditors (contributors to the social content sharing site Reddit) saw the *Kitchen Nightmares* episode and well, the rest is history. It was featured as a "what not to do" story on Mashable, *The Huffington Post*, and many other well known media sites. What ensued in ALL CAPS can only be described as the ultimate "what not to do in social media" lesson for every business on Earth.

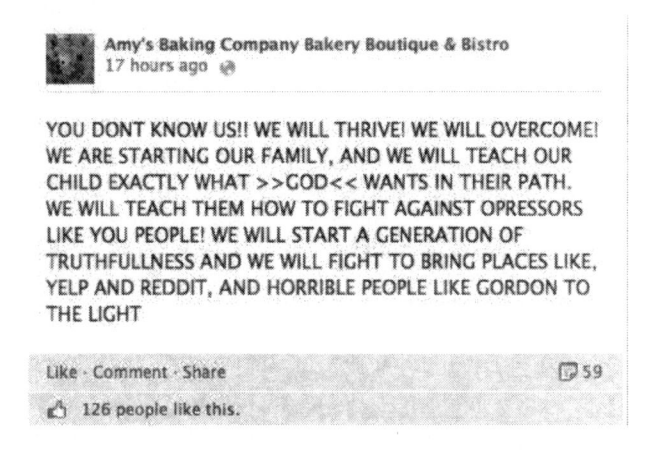

> **Amy's Baking Company Bakery Boutique & Bistro**
> 17 hours ago
>
> YOU DONT KNOW US!! WE WILL THRIVE! WE WILL OVERCOME! WE ARE STARTING OUR FAMILY, AND WE WILL TEACH OUR CHILD EXACTLY WHAT >>GOD<< WANTS IN THEIR PATH. WE WILL TEACH THEM HOW TO FIGHT AGAINST OPRESSORS LIKE YOU PEOPLE! WE WILL START A GENERATION OF TRUTHFULLNESS AND WE WILL FIGHT TO BRING PLACES LIKE, YELP AND REDDIT, AND HORRIBLE PEOPLE LIKE GORDON TO THE LIGHT
>
> Like · Comment · Share   59
> 126 people like this.

Owners Samy and Amy Bouzaglo's Facebook rant went on for hours, finally stopping after they said they have "God on their side." Some called this exchange the "most epic brand meltdown on Facebook ever." The owners eventually claimed that their Facebook, Yelp, Twitter accounts and website were all hacked and that they were working with local authorities to find the culprits.

SHEER ADVICE: HOW YOU CAN DO IT RIGHT

Take your fingers out of your ears. As we've been drilling into your head, LISTENING is one of the most critical aspects of social media and online marketing, and to ensuring that your brand is seen as authentic.

Social media monitoring tools such as HootSuite, Twitscoop, Facebook Insights, Google Analytics, and Social Mention can help you closely monitor your brand in social channels. Using a social media monitoring service such as Radian6 or Sysomos can also be really useful in helping you manage all of your social media sites so you always know what is being said about your brand, in real time.

Don't ignore. Stop ignoring the negative comments; they almost never go away, and can often snowball out of your control unless you intervene.

If people are genuinely engaged with your brand, engage with them back ... isn't that the point of "social" media? People want to know there are people behind every brand who might even make mistakes sometimes. Human mistakes are usually more forgiven than big cold corporations with no personal touch.

Speak up — sincerely. Lose the canned responses. Be real, polite, and authentic, and people will respect you for it.

Bite your tongue. You might want to fly off the handle when someone posts a scathing or untrue review about your brand, but take a step back and think about your response instead of firing back an emotional one instantly. Chances are if you go back and read your initial response after cooling off, you will tone it down ... possibly a lot.

Keep your cool and keep your response simple, honest, and polite (but not overly canned). Anyone posting an online review is a vocal customer. So, if you respond in a condescending or disingenuous way, there's a chance that reviewer could make the situation worse by posting your message all over the Internet — and fast (remember Amy's Baking Company)! So, take a deep breath and thank your reviewer for the business and the feedback. Negative reviews can shine the light on areas where improvements to your business need to be made.

Make sure your CAPS LOCK is off. Writing in ALL CAPS online is the equivalent of shouting like a maniac at someone.

Don't take it personally. We know it's hard when someone says something negative about your business, which is like someone bashing your kids. For founders and sole proprietors, it often feels like a personal attack. But as much as you may hate it, the review is feedback. Use that constructive criticism to improve your experience for the next customer.

Ask for a second chance. By contacting a negative reviewer (most online review sites give you that option) and establishing a conversation with them, you might be able to improve the situation and even change their mind about your business in the process. Customers want to know they are being heard. We've seen many negative reviews amended after the reviewer was contacted by the business and, accordingly, gave the business a second chance.

Accentuate the positive. Let reviewers know if you've made any changes or improvements as a result of their feedback, and thank them. It's important to share the fact that you've taken their feedback seriously and have taken positive steps as a result.

Focus on good customer service upfront. Great online content and reviews don't just happen for the sake of it. Empower your staff and have a system in place for dealing with every type of customer issue and complaint, because that is your opportunity to turn a two star review into one with glowing praise.

You can impact your brand's positive reputation online, and via word of mouth, if you have an honest approach. Remember, while responding to one reviewer, thousands of others may be silently watching, reading your comments, and taking note, forming their own opinions. These reviews live online for a long time. Make sure everything you put out there shows that you're a respectful, attentive, and honest business.

CLEAR CONCLUSION

No matter how transparent you are, you can't control everything that's said about your brand online. Still, honesty is the key to creating trust with people. Breaking that trust by not responding or trying to hide negative information will diminish your reputation and result in a loss of business. Acknowledging negative comments will actually enable you to increase customer loyalty and let customers see you in a bright, honest light — flaws and all.

Final Thoughts

It's hard to figure out who you are as a company and a person. It takes commitment and confidence to be authentic and a change maker, not just someone who jumps on trends and does what society and culture expects you to do. Being who you are, even as a brand, without fear of judgment, takes courage and fortitude.

Because of the increasing amount of information available to us through technology and the media, the desire for transparency is not going away. The current backlash against corporate America epitomizes the consumer's desire for honesty and ethics in business. For proof, look at the greater demands for organic products, the outcries against GMOs, and the insistence on products that don't destroy our health and planet — these are becoming the dominant voices in the market. As demand for the truth continues, companies that don't deliver will be called out for it. The more informed we become as a society, the more we will expect from businesses and brands in the form of honesty and engagement.

Take this consumer craving for authenticity to explore your own history, relationships with clients and consumers, and mission statement to find the exciting stories from within that you want to share. Discovering these stories, and telling them in the right places, at the right times, to the right people, will help you connect through actionable content that has a purpose. Once the "sell" is removed from your messaging, your authority and trustworthiness will increase … and so will the growth to your bottom line. Happy storytelling! Remember, the best stories are true.

References

Chapter 1
1) Stanford, Duane. "Equal Maker Hopes New Sales Strategy Proves Sweet." Bloomberg *Businessweek*, April 28, 2011.
http://buswk.co/ikQQpv
2) Roberts, Kevin. *Lovemarks: The Future Beyond Brands*. PowerHouse Books, 2005.

Chapter 2
1) Lecinski, Jim. *Winning the Zero Moment of Truth*. A Google 2011 ebook.
http://www.zeromomentoftruth.com/
2) Gutman, Brandon. "GE, General Mills and Sears Explain Their Success in Content Marketing (Part 2)." Forbes.com, May 17, 2012.
http://onforb.es/138iaxo/
3) Garrett, Jesse James. *The Elements of User Experience*, Second Edition. New Riders, 2010.
4) Karjaluoto, Eric. *Speak Human*. SmashLAB, 2009.
5) 2013 State of Inbound Marketing Annual Report. HubSpot.
http://bit.ly/11QEGKY

Chapter 3
1) The Naked Brand. Dir. Jeff Rosenblum and Sherng-Lee Huang. A Questus Production. 2013. Film.
http://thenakedbrand.com
2) Ibid.
3) Sauer, Abe. "Zappos Brand Returns to Form." Brand Channel, March 12, 2010.
http://bit.ly/13FiCL4
4) Wentz, Laurel. "Cannes' First Branded Content Grand Prix Goes to Chipotle." *Ad Age*, June 23, 2012.
http://bit.ly/OaGQ7r
5) "The Grape-Nuts Story: A Part of History." Web page.
http://www.postfoods.com/our-brands/grape-nuts/our-story/
6) Elliott, Stuart. "Grape-Nuts Wants You to Climb Every Mountain." *The New York Times*, May 28, 2013.
http://nyti.ms/ZcxfAF
7) Drell, Lauren. "Why Holstee's Sustainable Approach to Ecommerce Works." Mashable, May 8, 2012.
http://mashable.com/2012/05/08/holstee-video/
8) Scott, David Meerman. *The New Rules of Marketing & PR*. Your Coach In A Box, 2009.
9) "2013 B2B Content Marketing Benchmarks, Budgets and Trends — North America." Content Marketing Institute/Marketing Profs, sponsored by Brightcove.
http://bit.ly/PNPwko

Chapter 4

1) Huba, Jackie and McConnell, Ben. *Creating Customer Evangelists*. Dearborn Trade Publishing, 2003.
2) Collier, Mack. "Four Ways to Create an Army of Fans for Your Brand." MarketingProfs.com, April 15, 2013.
http://bit.ly/XMLlVu
3) Ewing, Mike. "71% More Likely to Purchase Based on Social Media Referrals [Infographic]." January 9, 2012.
http://bit.ly/AoolAI
4) "Marketing Without Fingerprints." Church of the Customer Podcast. January 10, 2006.
http://bit.ly/157M1ZU
5) Dilworth, Dianna. "Turning Loyal Customers Into Brand Evangelists." *Direct Marketing News*, May 1, 2013.
http://bit.ly/10W1CP3
6) Dan, Avi. "Writing An Awesome Letter To A 7-Year Old, And Gaining A Lifetime Customer For LEGO." Forbes.com, January 14, 2013.
http://onforb.es/ZPj2X4
7) Godin, Seth. *Linchpin*. Penguin Group, 2011.
8) Phillips, Robbin, Cordell, Greg, Church, Geno, and Jones, Spike. *Brains on Fire*. John Wiley & Sons, Inc., 2010.
9) Burlingham, Bo. "The Coolest Small Company in America." *Inc.*, January 1, 2003.
http://www.inc.com/magazine/20030101/25036.html
10) "25 of the World's Best Food Markets." *Food & Wine*, April 2004.
http://bit.ly/5o52i
11) Ovsey, Dan. "Authenticity Key Ingredient in Recipe to Produce Employee Evangelists." *Financial Post*, August 1, 2012.
http://bit.ly/OGFzCU
12) "Socially Awkward Media." A.T. Kearney.
http://bit.ly/RJfsue

Chapter 5

1) "Socially Awkward Media." A.T. Kearney.
http://bit.ly/RJfsue
2) The Naked Brand. Dir. Jeff Rosenblum and Sherng-Lee Huang. A Questus Production. 2013. Film.
http://thenakedbrand.com
3) Hernandez, Brian Anthony. "KitchenAid Tweets Joke About Obama's Dead Grandma [Updated]." Mashable, October 3, 2012.
http://on.mash.to/RBV9B8
4) Manker, Rob. "Subway Footlong Lawsuits: Sandwich Chain Responds." *Chicago Tribune*, January 24, 2013.
http://bit.ly/18dzjyB
5) "A Letter to Our Guests." Lululemon.com, March 18, 2013.
http://bit.ly/WzOR8h

About the Authors

Dechay Watts

Dechay is the co-founder and chief strategy officer at SPROUT Content, where she applies her stellar listening and observational skills to filter through the noise and create concise and strategic plans for clients.

After graduating from the University of Florida, Dechay left the Sunshine State for the Empire State where she launched a career in PR, working in a division of Saatchi & Saatchi (and where she fatefully met co-author and business partner Debbie Williams). She worked in New York for several years before her travel bug took over and led her on a journey across the country, then through most of Europe, before heading back to the white sands of the Florida Gulf Coast. Dechay worked for the first local Internet startup in the area, then helped email security company AppRiver become one of *Inc.'s* Fastest Growing Companies in the U.S. as its director of marketing. Always following her inner compass, she was led down an entrepreneurial path to start her own web content development company, Watts Writing Studio, which planted the seeds for SPROUT Content.

Dechay is an active volunteer, supporting Big Brothers Big Sisters, Think Beyond, and IMPACT 100. She now lives in Denver with her husband Rich, Sophie (the lab they purposefully brought home), and "Little Dog" Maggie who decided to live with them and never leave. Dechay earned a BA in Journalism from the University of Florida and an MBA from the University of West Florida.

Learn more about SPROUT Content at www.sproutcontent.com, and find Dechay on Twitter @Dechay.

Debbie Williams

Debbie is the co-founder and chief content officer at SPROUT Content, where she brings her passion for revealing the most unique plot lines of a brand story and eloquently capturing the spirit and emotion of brands through words to all SPROUT Content clients.

After working for several years in the PR agency world in New York (where she met co-author and business partner Dechay Watts), Debbie found her calling as a copywriter and launched a successful 10-year career working for top agencies and brands including beauty.com, Grey Advertising, *Good Housekeeping Magazine*, LVMH Fragrance Brands, and KAO Brands Co.

Born and raised in New Jersey, a stone's throw from NYC, Debbie is a city girl at heart who never imagined herself anywhere else. But life, fate, and love takes you to strange places, and she's all the better for it. After meeting her husband at Dechay's wedding in Florida, she traded city streets for white sands and now calls the Gulf Coast home. Debbie lives in Pensacola with her husband and two daughters.

Debbie earned a BA in English from Seton Hall University. She is a contributor to the Content Marketing Institute blog and MarketingProfs blog, and has spoken at Content Marketing World.

Learn more about SPROUT Content at www.sproutcontent.com, and find Debbie on Twitter @debwilliams23.

Said Baaghil

Raised in North Africa, Europe, and the United States, Said attended the University of Maine at Machias where he earned a BS in Marketing.

After working in corporate America for 10 years, Said saw a great need for brand marketing expertise in the Middle East and Asia and launched his consultancy there in 2000. Since then, he has helped dozens of brands worldwide with his strategic and passionate approach to brand marketing. Through his practice, AskBaaghil.com, Said offers online and in-person brand marketing consultation.

Said is a sought-after speaker and is co-author of the books *The Power of Belonging, Eccentric Marketing, Brand Revolution,* and *Glamour Globals.* Said often lives in Jeddah, Saudi Arabia, and Hong Kong, but he's rarely "home" for long, and is a citizen of the world. Said's "boss," Rakun Said Baaghil, is his real inspiration.

Find Said online at askbaaghil.com or on Twitter @baaghil.

Content Marketing Institute Titles

Managing Content Marketing
The Real-World Guide for Creating Passionate Subscribers to Your Brand
By Robert Rose & Joe Pulizzi

Capturing Community
Build, Manage, and Market Your Online Community
By Michael Silverman

Bold Brand
The New Rules for Differentiating, Branding, and Marketing Your Professional Services Firm
By Josh Miles

Your Customer Creation Equation
Unexpected Website Formulas of the Conversion Scientist™
By Brian Massey

Brandscaping
Unleashing the Power of Partnerships
By Andrew M. Davis

The Marketer's Guide to SlideShare
How to Build Your Brand, Generate Leads & Create Opportunities
By Todd Wheatland

Brands in Glass Houses
How to Embrace Transparency & Grow Your Business Through Content Marketing
By Dechay Watts and Debbie Williams with Said Baaghil

Content Marketing Institute books are available at special quantity discounts to use as premiums and sales promotions, or for use in corporate training programs. To place a bulk order, please contact the Content Marketing Institute at info@contentinstitute.com or 888/554-2014.
www.contentmarketinginstitute.com

CPSIA information can be obtained at www.ICGtesting.com
Printed in the USA
LVOW12s2203250214

375208LV00014B/353/P